MODERN TIMES

General Editor: John Robottom

Roosevelt and the United States

Second Edition

G000022525

D. B. O'Callaghan

Longman
London and New York

Contents

1
Beginnings

Childhood

Seventy-five miles to the north of the city of New York, on a wooded hill high above the Hudson River, stands a large old country house named Hyde Park. Late in the evening of a cold and windy January day in the year 1882 the owner of the house, a side-whiskered New York businessman named James Roosevelt, took out a diary and proudly wrote in it: 'At quarter to nine my Sallie had a splendid large baby boy. He weighs nine pounds without clothes.' That 'large baby boy' was destined to become the most loved – and possibly the most hated – of all American Presidents. He was christened a few weeks later – Franklin Delano Roosevelt.

Growing up

The world which Franklin Roosevelt entered on that winter's evening in 1882 was secure and comfortable. His father was wealthy man who owned an estate of hundreds of hectares of farmland and forest around the house at Hyde Park and also had an interest in a number of thriving business companies.

Most of Franklin's childhood was spent at Hyde Park, and among the woods and fields of the Hudson valley he grew to love the countryside. In September 1896, however, his parents sent him to Groton, a boarding school for boys from wealthy families which had recently been set up in New England.

Peabody and Groton

Groton's headmaster was Endicott Peabody, a big, athletic young clergyman. His aim was to make Groton into an American version of such English public schools as Eton, which prepared boys from wealthy families to take over the future leadership of their country. Peabody attached particular importance to character training. He insisted that his pupils should learn to stand on their own feet and not expect to go through life being pampered just because their parents were wealthy. They had to learn, too, that people with the good fortune to be born wealthy had a duty to try to be of service to their country and their less fortunate fellow citizens.

Franklin Roosevelt was never one of Peabody's best pupils. In class he was usually between sixth and tenth and he never shone at sport. But Peabody's idea that the wealthy had a duty to serve their country made a lasting impression upon him.

The Harvard years

In the summer of 1900 the eighteen-year-old Franklin Roosevelt left Groton and enrolled as a student at Harvard University, the American equivalent of the English universities of Oxford and Cambridge.

The Crimson

He decided to specialise in the study of history and government. But he wanted to enjoy himself at Harvard, too. He joined the Fly, the most fashionable student club. He also told his parents that he intended to try to get a position on the student newspaper, *The Crimson*. With typical optimism he added '. . . and if I work hard for two years I may be made an editor'.

A few years later this forecast came true. After working hard as a reporter the young Roosevelt was made an assistant editor on the paper. The following year he became its editor-in-chief.

The young reformer

An interesting change took place in *The Crimson* during the time that Franklin Roosevelt held this position. The paper had always taken a very respectful attitude towards the University authorities. Now it began to prod them, politely but firmly, to make improvements. Roosevelt wrote, for example, that the fire escapes in the students' dormitories ought to be improved before there was a serious accident.

The young editor also criticised the students for their lack of interest in the elections to choose the officials who ran student affairs. The results of such elections were usually decided by the members of the fashionable clubs like the Fly who would simply vote for one of their friends. Since many other students never bothered to vote at all, the candidates favoured by the clubs would usually be elected. This was wrong, declared Roosevelt. He urged all those entitled to a vote to use their right, so that the officials elected would be the true choice of all the students.

The reforms with which Roosevelt was concerned in *The Crimson* were, of course, small ones compared with the problems of the outside world. His basic attitude, however – the desire to change and to improve rather than to accept things as they were – foreshadowed that which he would adopt in later years towards much greater problems.

Eleanor

Two important events in Franklin Roosevelt's personal life occurred while he was at Harvard. While he was in his first year his father died. During his last year he fell in love. The girl's name was Eleanor – Eleanor Roosevelt, the niece of Theodore Roosevelt, Franklin's own

The young Roosevelts at Hyde Park in the early years of their marriage. A solemn Franklin holds the knitting while Eleanor looks amused.

distant relative and at that time the President of the United States. Eleanor was three years younger than Franklin, a tall, shy girl with an expressive face and beautiful eyes. Although she and Franklin had met occasionally when they were children, it was not until Franklin was in his third year at Harvard that they began to see each other more often. Eleanor was then eighteen and had just returned home from three years at school in England.

Marriage

Franklin was more and more attracted to his cousin. He took her to football matches and met her at dances and dinners. Finally, late in 1903, he asked her to marry him and she agreed.

Since Eleanor was an orphan, it was arranged that the wedding should take place at the home of her cousin in New York. Her uncle Theodore agreed to give her away, and on the day of the wedding the house was besieged by crowds of people eager to see the President. A great cheer arose when he drove up in an open carriage, waving his top hat and flashing a toothy smile to acknowledge the crowd. The arrival of the bridegroom a few moments later passed almost unnoticed!

After honeymooning in Europe the young couple settled into their first home, a twelve-foot-wide house in New York, and Franklin began studying to become a lawyer. All the signs seemed to indicate that the future would be secure and comfortable – but perhaps rather dull.

2

A Changing Land

Industry and immigrants

What sort of country was the United States of America when Franklin Roosevelt married his cousin in the spring of 1904?

Industrial growth

Perhaps its most striking feature was the speed at which industry had grown in recent years. Fifty years earlier the United States had been mainly a farming country. But since then vast new deposits of raw materials of many kinds had been discovered and developed. The output of coal and iron – the most vital of all industrial raw materials – had risen especially fast. By 1900 the output of coal was nine times higher than it had been in 1860, while that of iron was twenty times higher.

Growing cities

These and other raw materials had made possible a rapid growth of manufacturing industries in the United States. As these industries grew, more and more people became city dwellers, for the new factories of cities such as Pittsburgh and Chicago needed workers in ever increasing numbers

Immigrants

Some of these new city dwellers were Americans, drawn from the countryside by the promise of higher wages. Many others were immigrants from other countries who were attracted to America in their millions in these years by the hope of a better life in a new land.

Ellis Island

So many immigrants wanted to enter the United States, especially from southern and eastern Europe, that the government found it difficult to keep check on them. To control the situation, in 1892 it opened a special place of entry in New York harbour. This place was called Ellis Island. All intending immigrants were examined there before they were allowed to enter.

During its busiest times Ellis Island dealt with almost 2,000 immigrants a day. Between its opening and 1954, when it closed its doors, more than 20 million people waited anxiously in its halls and corridors. Immigration officers asked them questions to find out if they were criminals or mentally abnormal. Doctors examined them for disease.

'People from other countries were attracted to America in their millions.' Immigrants from Europe land at Ellis Island in the early years of the twentieth century.

A letter chalked on their clothing – H for heart disease or E for eye disease – could end their hopes of a new life in America.

But most passed the examinations. Almost half of all present-day Americans have ancestors who entered the United States by way of Ellis Island. One day in the 1970s one such American, a man named Leon Stein, stood in Ellis Island's echoing, empty Great Hall and spoke quietly of the way it made him feel:

> 'My parents came through this place at the turn of the century. How can I stand here and not be moved? I feel it is haunted. I think if you become really quiet you can actually hear all the crying, all the feeling, all the impatience, all the misunderstanding that went on in this hall. Being born again is not an easy thing and the people who came through here were being born again. This was their gateway to hope, to a new life.'
>
> Leon Stein quoted in Desmond Wilcox, *Americans*, 1978.

Immigrant life

The immigrants found work in busy cities like New York, Chicago and Pittsburgh – stitching garments, feeding furnaces, labouring on factory assembly lines, hacking out coal. For most immigrants this new life was a hard one. They were outsiders in a strange land. Often they could not even speak its language. Only the hardest and lowest paid jobs were open to them. To survive they often had to work for long hours in dangerous conditions and to live in over-crowded slums that were breeding places of disease and misery.

The attractions of America

Yet, bad as conditions were, they often seemed preferable to those that the immigrants had left behind. In the United States they were free from religious and political persecution. They were often better dressed and better fed than they had ever been before. They marvelled at such wonders as free schools for their children; at lamps glowing along city streets at night; and at the fact that soap was cheap enough to be used by everyone! So the immigrants continued to pour in. By 1910 it was estimated that 14.5 per cent of the people then living in the United States had been born in other countries.

Trusts, muckrakers and Progressives

By 1890 the industries of the United States were earning the country more than its farmlands. In the twenty years that followed, industrial output went on growing. By 1913 more than a third of the whole world's industrial production was pouring from the mines and factories of the United States.

Capitalists

The growth of American industry was organised and controlled by 'capitalists' – businessmen who found the money to set up mines, factories and trading businesses. Many of these men began their lives in poverty, but by a mixture of hard work, ability and ruthless disregard for the rights of others, they made themselves wealthy and powerful. Their admirers called such men 'captains of industry'. Their critics called them 'robber barons' – or worse!

Andrew Carnegie

Andrew Carnegie was one of the best known. Carnegie was born in Scotland in 1835, but emigrated to America at the age of thirteen. He began his life there working for one dollar twenty cents a week in a Pittsburgh cotton mill. From there he moved to a job in a telegraph office, then to one on the Pennsylvania Railroad. By the time he was thirty he already had an income of over forty thousand dollars a year from far-sighted investments.

Carnegie concentrated his investments in the iron and steel business. By the 1860s he controlled companies making bridges, rails and locomotives for the railroads. In the 1870s he built the biggest steel mill in America in Pennsylvania. He also owned coal and iron ore mines, a fleet of steam ships and his own railroad.

Nothing like Carnegie's wealth and industrial power had ever before been seen in the United States. By 1900, as owner of half the shares in the giant Carnegie Steel Corporation, his annual income was estimated to be over twenty-three million dollars – this was about *twenty thousand* times more than the income of the average American of the day.

Corporations and trusts

The great wealth of men like Carnegie came partly from their success in swallowing up rival firms or driving them out of business. Carnegie and other businessmen such as John D. Rockefeller, the 'king' of the growing oil industry, realised that by doing this they could greatly increase their profits.

The giant industrial organisations that such men created were known as 'corporations'. Sometimes corporations were grouped together to form 'trusts', organisations which were bigger and more powerful still. By the early twentieth century trusts controlled large parts of American industry. One controlled steel, another oil, another meat-packing, and there were many more. The biggest trusts were richer than most of the world's nations. By their wealth and power – and especially their power to decide wages and prices – they controlled the lives of millions.

The power of the trusts

Many Americans were alarmed by the power of the trusts. The United States was a land that was supposed to offer equal opportunities to everyone. Yet now, it seemed, the country was coming under the control of a handful of rich and powerful men who were able to do more or less what they wished. Some bribed politicians to pass laws which favoured them. Others hired private armies to crush attempts by their workers to obtain better conditions. Their attitude to the rights of others was summed up in a famous remark of the railroad 'king', William H. Vanderbilt. When asked whether he thought railroads should be run in the public interest, he replied 'The public be damned!'

The contemptuous way in which leaders of industry like Vanderbilt rejected criticism strengthened the feeling that something ought to be done to limit the growing power of such men. Many people came to see this as the most important problem facing the United States in the early years of the twentieth century.

Muckrakers

A stream of books and magazine articles drew attention to this and other national problems. Some dealt with conditions of life in the slums of the great cities, some with bribery and corruption in government,

'By their wealth and power they controlled the lives of millions.' A late nineteenth century cartoon shows workers, farmers and the owners of small businesses bowing down before the might of the trusts.

HISTORY REPEATS ITSELF. THE ROBBER BARONS OF THE MIDDLE AGES AND THE ROBBER BARONS OF TO-DAY.

others with the dishonesty of wealthy businessmen. They often revealed startling and shocking facts. This caused some critics of the authors to describe them as 'muckrakers'.

The Jungle

One of the best known muckrakers was Upton Sinclair. In 1906 Sinclair attacked the meat-packing industry in his novel *The Jungle*. This gave a horrifying description of the slaughter houses of Chicago:

> 'These rats were nuisances and the packers put out poisoned bread for them; they would die and then rats, bread and meat would go into the hoppers together. The meat would be shovelled into carts and the man who did the shovelling did not trouble to lift a rat out even when he saw one.'
>
> Upton Sinclair, *The Jungle*, 1906.

The Jungle horrified middle-class Americans. They were even more horrified when government inspectors confirmed that most of what Sinclair had written was true. Meat sales dropped by half. The meat companies begged the government to inspect their premises in order to convince people that their products were fit to eat. Congress quickly passed a new federal meat-inspection law.

Progressives

Demands began to grow that the nation's leaders should deal with other scandals exposed by the muckrakers. This pressure brought about an important change in American political life. Before 1900 most Americans believed in 'laissez faire' – the idea that governments should interfere with business, and people's lives generally, as little as possible. After 1900 many became 'Progressives'. A Progressive was someone who believed that, where necessary, the government should take action to deal with the problems of society.

American government

The President

In the United States of America one person – the President – occupies a position carrying powers and responsibilities which in Britain are divided between two persons, the monarch and the Prime Minister. Like the British monarch, he is the state's official head and is intended to be a kind of living symbol of the nation's traditions. But in addition, like the British Prime Minister, he is in control of the actual running of his country's affairs; in other words, he is the head of the 'executive' side of the national, or 'Federal', government.

The President plays the main part in deciding the policies of the United States government and chooses the people (known as 'Secretaries') who run its various departments. He also makes treaties with other countries and is the Commander-in-Chief of the nation's armed forces. He is the most powerful elected leader in the world.

Congress

Yet, great as the American President's powers are, they are not unlimited. For one thing, although the President can suggest new laws, he

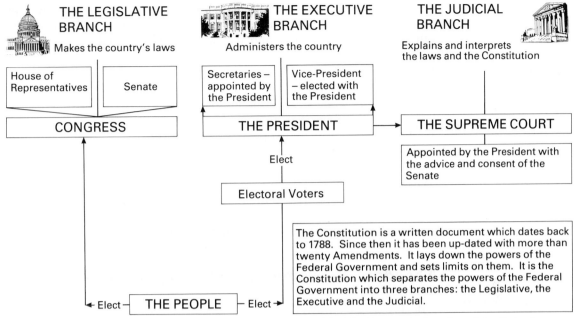

THE LEGISLATIVE BRANCH
Makes the country's laws

House of Representatives	Senate

CONGRESS

THE EXECUTIVE BRANCH
Administers the country

Secretaries – appointed by the President	Vice-President – elected with the President

THE PRESIDENT

Elect

Electoral Voters

THE JUDICIAL BRANCH
Explains and interprets the laws and the Constitution

THE SUPREME COURT

Appointed by the President with the advice and consent of the Senate

The Constitution is a written document which dates back to 1788. Since then it has been up-dated with more than twenty Amendments. It lays down the powers of the Federal Government and sets limits on them. It is the Constitution which separates the powers of the Federal Government into three branches: the Legislative, the Executive and the Judicial.

← Elect — THE PEOPLE — Elect →

How the United States is governed (1). The three main branches of the Federal government.

cannot make laws himself. The American Constitution – that is, the set of rules for carrying on the government of the United States – gives this law making, or legislative, power to Congress, as the American parliament is known.

Congress consists of two parts – the Senate and the House of Representatives. Both are made up of members chosen by the people of the various states which together make up the United States. The number of members a particular state has in the House of Representatives depends upon its population. A thickly-peopled state like New York has forty-one, while one with a comparatively small population like Delaware has only one. In the Senate, however, each state is equally represented, with two members regardless of its population. In order to govern successfully a President must be able to persuade Congress to pass the laws that he believes the nation needs.

The Supreme Court

In addition to the President and Congress, the Federal government of the United States has a third part. This is the Supreme Court, which limits the powers of the other two. Any laws agreed by Congress and the President have to meet certain conditions set out in the Constitution. Deciding whether they do so is the job of the Supreme Court. If the Supreme Court decides that a law does *not* meet the Constitution's conditions, it has the power to declare that law illegal.

The States

As well as being limited by Congress and the Supreme Court, the powers of the President are also limited by the fact that the United States is a 'federation' – that is, a single nation which has been forged out of a number of separate states. These states differ greatly in size, in population, in economic life and each has its own system of laws, its own official head or Governor and its own elected law-making body.

State governments

Under the American Constitution, the individual state governments have very considerable powers. At the beginning of the twentieth century these powers were even greater than they are now. The state governments controlled most matters which particularly concerned their own state and its people – education, health, working conditions and so on. Generally speaking, only matters which concerned the country as a whole were dealt with by the national government in Washington. These included such things as the nation's defence and its relations with other countries. Most other matters were left to the state governments, which jealously guarded their rights against any attempt by the Federal government to interfere with them.

Theodore Roosevelt and 'The Square Deal'

The Progressive movement found a leader in the Republican politician Theodore Roosevelt. Franklin and Eleanor Roosevelt's 'Uncle Teddy' became President in 1901. One of his main beliefs was that the President should use the power of the Federal government to see that the ordinary man and woman got what he called 'a square deal'.

Roosevelt and the trusts

Roosevelt was particularly concerned about the power of the trusts. His idea was to give the United States the best of both worlds. He wanted to allow businessmen enough freedom of action to make their firms efficient and prosperous, but at the same time to prevent them from taking unfair advantage of other people. In 1905 a humourist made fun of this two-sided attitude by describing it in these words:

> 'Th' thrusts are heejous monsthers built up by the inlightened intherprise ov th' men that have done so much to advance progress in our beloved counthry. On wan hand I wud stamp them undher fut, on th' other hand, not so fast'
> 'Mr Deeley', a fictional character created by Finley Peter Dunne.

A dispute involving the big railroad companies provided an example of the 'square deal' in action. Roosevelt forced them to charge all their customers fair rates, instead of allowing large customers like the oil and meat-packing trusts to pay less than farmers and small businesses.

Protection and conservation

Roosevelt also supported laws which compelled manufacturers of foods and medicines to make sure that their products were pure. But perhaps his most important service to his country was to persuade Congress to pass a number of conservation laws. These were laws to save the natural resources of the United States from being exploited carelessly and greedily. They protected millions of hectares of land and preserved their forest and mineral wealth for the use of future generations.

3

The Apprentice Politician

Choosing a party

Republican or Democrat?

Franklin Roosevelt admired 'Uncle Teddy' for his attempts to control big business and for his policies of social reform. Before long he began to consider giving up his work as a lawyer in order to make a career for himself in politics.

He did not feel, however, that he could follow Teddy's example and enter politics as a member of the Republican party. For one thing, his own branch of the Roosevelt family had long been supporters of the Democrats, the United States' other main political party. More important than this, though, Franklin did not agree with the ideas of many Republicans.

The 'Old Guard'

As we have seen, Theodore Roosevelt was a Progressive Republican, who believed that the United States needed reforming and changing. However, many Republicans disliked his policies, and only supported him because of his great popularity with the voters. These 'Old Guard' Republicans believed that action by the Federal government, particularly in anything concerning the control of industry and trade, should be kept to a minimum.

Distrust of government

This distrust of 'strong' Federal government was, and still is, deep rooted in the United States. It comes partly from the desire of the individual states to run their own affairs, and partly from a fear of government interference with the rights of the individual. The distrust is further strengthened by a belief that it is largely by the efforts of individuals that the United States has grown into a powerful and prosperous nation. So although a majority of Americans in the early 1900s were sympathetic towards the ideas of the President, there was a good deal of support, too, for the 'Old Guard' point of view.

When Theodore Roosevelt retired as President in 1909 and went off to Africa to hunt big game, these Old Guard sympathisers sighed with relief. At last they were rid of 'the Wild Man', as some of them called him. None of them knew that as one troublesome Roosevelt was leaving the political stage, another, who would eventually prove even more troublesome, was preparing to make his entrance.

The Democratic candidate

Franklin Roosevelt entered politics in 1910. His chance came when leaders of the Democratic party in Dutchess County, the part of New York State where Hyde Park was situated, asked him if he would become their candidate in the forthcoming election to choose a new State Senator for the district. From their point of view the young Roosevelt was in many ways an ideal candidate. He had a famous name, an attractive appearance and personality, and was fairly well known locally. In addition, he was rich enough to be able to pay his own election expenses!

Franklin Roosevelt decided to accept and immediately began a whirlwind election campaign. For many years the people of the district in which he was running for election had voted for a Republican to represent them in the State Senate. Roosevelt knew that if he was going to win he would have to work hard to persuade them to vote for him. This would not be easy for many of the voters lived on lonely farms or in isolated villages.

Campaigning in style

To get round to see as many voters as possible Roosevelt hired a car, a bright red tourer without either top or windscreen, which he named 'the Red Peril'. Some of his friends advised him not to use it, since cars at this time were generally disliked by country folk because of the way they scared horses and cattle with their clattering and banging.

Franklin Roosevelt ignored their warnings. Throughout the campaign the Red Peril, decked out with flags and with its polished brass headlamps gleaming, chugged and backfired its way all over the district.

Roosevelt gave as many as twenty speeches in a day. He gave them in town halls, in schools, from the back of the car and even from the tops of haystacks. He was so keen that on one occasion he and his party strayed by mistake over the border from New York into the neighbouring state of Connecticut, and he found himself addressing a crowd which couldn't vote for him anyway. Despite such mishaps, to the surprise of both his supporters and his opponents Franklin Roosevelt won the election.

The state senator

In 1911 Franklin Roosevelt took his place in the New York Senate at the state's capital city of Albany, some miles up the Hudson river from his home at Hyde Park. It soon became clear that this lean, handsome 'college kid', as some of the older politicians patronizingly called him, had a mind of his own and no intention of obediently doing what he was told by the Democratic party leaders. In fact, within weeks of his election he was taking part in a rebellion against them.

Tammany Hall   The Democratic party in New York State was largely controlled by a group of professional politicians who ran the party in the city of New York. These men belonged to a political organisation, or 'machine', known as Tammany Hall. Many of them did not hold elected offices themselves, but they were very powerful behind the scenes in politics.

The power of the Tammany Hall political 'bosses' came from their ability to persuade people to vote for the party's candidates. They gained the gratitude of the city's poor by finding them jobs when they were out of work, providing them with free coal in winter, and giving free shoes to their children. In return for such favours the bosses expected their followers to vote in elections for the candidate they had chosen. Their own reward came later. From any candidate who was elected with their support the bosses expected favours for themselves – such as well-paid jobs at the government's expense or profitable business contracts.

Electing a senator   The struggle with the bosses in which Franklin Roosevelt was involved arose over the election of a senator to represent New York State in the United States Senate in Washington. As we have seen, each state was entitled to send two senators to Washington, and the position was one of great honour and influence. In 1911 these United States senators were not elected directly by the people, but by a vote amongst the

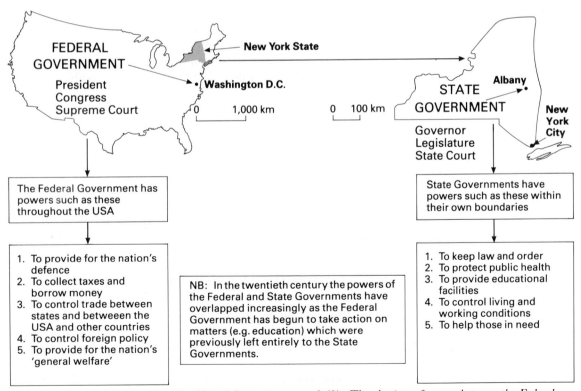

How the United States is governed (2). The sharing of power between the Federal government and the governments of the individual states.

members of the Assembly of the state which they were to represent.

The Democratic party bosses in New York had already decided upon their man, a wealthy businessman named Sheehan. His election seemed certain, for the Democrats had a large enough majority in the Assembly to ensure his success – providing that all the party's members voted as the bosses asked them to vote.

Opposing the bosses

But some Democrats did not agree with the choice. Franklin Roosevelt was one. How could a man like Sheehan be expected to take a sympathetic interest in the welfare of ordinary people?, he asked himself. He had too many links with big business. And what right had the party bosses to decide the matter anyway? There and then he decided to join forces with the handful of fellow Democrats who agreed with him, so that they could block Sheehan's election by refusing to vote for him.

The Sheehan affair

Roosevelt's Albany house became the headquarters of the small rebel group. For ten weeks they held out against all attempts by the party bosses to persuade them to vote for Sheehan. At last, after both threats and persuasion had failed, the bosses dropped Sheehan, put forward a candidate with more progressive views and the rebel group turned up and voted for him.

Changing the system

The Sheehan affair was important in a number of ways. For one thing, it helped to make the American system of government more democratic. In 1913 the country's Constitution was changed to make it possible for senators to be elected in future by a direct vote of the people of each state instead of by the State Assemblies – a reform for which progressives had been pressing for years. For another, it gave Franklin Roosevelt his first real taste of active political life – and he loved it. 'I never had as much fun in my life as I am having right now,' he told a reporter during the Sheehan struggle.

The appeal of politics

He meant it. He had fallen for the excitement of political life. He was fascinated, too, by the business of meeting all kinds of people and of trying to understand and reach agreement with them. Most of all he liked the sense of satisfaction which came from achieving a worthwhile aim. After this there was never any question in his mind as to what his career should be. There was only one thing for him – politics!

The birth of a practical politician

Roosevelt and the bosses

The Sheehan affair made Franklin Roosevelt a well known figure in New York State and the people of his district were proud of him. With the party bosses he was not so popular, for he continued to be too independent for their liking.

But, despite their dislike of one another, a grudging sort of mutual respect gradually grew up between Roosevelt and the bosses. The bosses realised that they had on their hands not just a rich man playing at politics, but a fighter; someone who might be persuaded, but whom it did not pay to try to push around. For his part, Roosevelt began to realise that politics was a far more complicated business than he had thought.

Learning the political trade

At first he tended to be obstinate and self-righteous. 'You know,' he said to a friend years later, 'I was an awfully mean cuss when I first went into politics.'

He matured fast though. He learned, for instance, that disagreements were not always simple matters of right or wrong, and that even in Tammany Hall there were honest men with good intentions. He learned, too, the value of compromising, of giving up one part of his aims in order to achieve the rest.

The practical politician

He learned this so well that in later years some people were to criticise him for being too ready to compromise. When he was President he was sometimes accused of deliberately turning a blind eye to the activities of dishonest and self-seeking politicians, and even of doing favours for them, in order to obtain their support for his policies.

To Roosevelt such criticisms seemed unrealistic. 'I do not choose the tools with which I must work,' he once said. While he preferred to work with honest politicians if he could, if the only way to pass good and necessary laws was to persuade corrupt politicians to vote for them, then he was willing to do this. Rightly or wrongly, this seemed to him preferable to not having the laws at all.

It was this man who began to be born during these years in the New York State Senate at Albany: a practical politician, who was learning how to work the complicated and sometimes dirty machinery of American politics superbly well in order to achieve his aims.

Wilson for President

Electing a President

The American Constitution lays down that a Presidential election must be held every four years. This happens early in the November of every leap year. The result of the election is not decided simply by counting up the votes to see which candidate has obtained the highest total in the country as a whole. Instead, Presidential elections are based upon what is known as the 'electoral college' system.

Under this system each state has a certain number of votes to cast in the Presidential election. The number of 'electoral votes' a state is entitled to have is calculated by adding together the number of Representatives and the number of Senators that it has in the two houses of Congress in Washington. This means that a state with a large population, like New York, has forty-three electoral votes, while a small state like Delaware has only three. Whichever candidate gains a majority of the individual votes cast in any one state, even if the majority is only a tiny one, wins all that state's electoral votes. And the candidate who gains the most electoral votes nation-wide wins the election.

'He declared that he would fight for the man who was knocking at the closed door of opportunity.' Woodrow Wilson is congratulated on being chosen as the Democratic party's candidate for the Presidency in the 1912 election.

The 1912 Presidential election

In 1912, for the first time for years, the Democrats had a good chance of winning the Presidential election, for a serious split had appeared in the ranks of the Republican party. The Old Guard Republicans had re-nominated the existing President Taft as their party's official candidate. But Progressive Republicans had not wanted Taft and had broken away from the Old Guard and chosen their own candidate – Theodore Roosevelt, who had returned from his foreign travels and was impatient to get back into action.

The probability that the votes of Republican supporters would be divided between Taft and Theodore Roosevelt made a Democratic victory in the 1912 election almost certain. This made it vitally important to Democrats who were interested in reform that their party should choose the right candidate.

Woodrow Wilson

The man upon whom Progressive Democrats had their eyes was Woodrow Wilson, the Governor of the state of New Jersey. Wilson had fought successfully to make sure that the government of New Jersey was run for the benefit of its people, reducing corruption and introducing such social reforms as laws to compensate workers for injuries at work. He declared that if he became President he would fight 'not for the man who has made good but for the man who is going to make good – the man who is knocking and fighting at the closed door of opportunity.'

Such words convinced Franklin Roosevelt and other Progressive Democrats that here was just the kind of man the country needed as its leader. But there was a difficulty. Although Progressive Democrats wanted Wilson, the party bosses didn't.

Wilson wins

In June, 1912, the Democratic party's National Convention – a meeting of party representatives from all over the country – met in Baltimore to choose the party's candidate for the Presidency. Roosevelt and other Progressives worked hard to sway opinion on to the side of Wilson. When the Convention began they dashed round meeting delegates from all over the country, pleading with them to vote for him. At last, after days of uncertainty, the Convention made its decision. It was Wilson, and when the Presidential election took place that autumn he was elected.

A job in Washington

Wilson was inaugurated – sworn-in – as President in the following March. On the morning of the ceremony Roosevelt ran into Josephus Daniels, a Carolina newspaper man whom Wilson had just appointed Secretary to the Navy. He congratulated Daniels and the older man looked at him quizzically.

'How would you like to come to Washington as Assistant Secretary of the Navy?' he asked.

Roosevelt jumped at the offer. 'It would please me better than anything in the world,' he replied.

Within a few days the offer had been officially confirmed by the President. Franklin Roosevelt resigned from his position as State Senator and on 17 March, 1913 – the eighth anniversary of his marriage to Eleanor – he was sworn-in to his new position.

4

The Wilson Years

Woodrow Wilson and 'The New Freedom'

Wilson's aims

In March 1913, Woodrow Wilson stood before the Capitol building in Washington and was sworn-in as President of the United States of America. Then, turning to the crowd which had gathered to watch the ceremony, he made a brief speech about the state of the country. This is part of what he said:

> 'We have built up a great system of government. But evil has come with the good ... We have squandered [wasted] a great part of what we might have used. We have been proud of our industrial achievements, but we have not hitherto stopped thoughtfully enough to count the human cost ...'
>
> President Woodrow Wilson, March 1913.

One of these 'human costs', Wilson believed, had been the near destruction for many Americans of a fair chance to get on in life. Despite Theodore Roosevelt's attempts to bring the trusts under control, they were even more powerful in 1913 than they had been in 1900. Workers, farmers, the owners of small businesses had seen their opportunities shrinking steadily, owing to the continuing growth of the power of 'big business' over the nation's economic life. Wilson believed that only prompt and vigorous action by the Federal government could halt this process. As President, he was determined to see that such action was taken.

'The New Freedom'

Wilson called his policies 'The New Freedom'. They were put into effect by a series of laws passed between 1913 and 1917. These laws further reduced the powers of the trusts, gave more rights to labour unions, and made it easier for farmers to borrow money from the Federal government to develop their land.

But not all Wilson's plans of reform were accepted. For example, the Senate refused to pass a law giving the federal authorities a certain amount of control over the buying and selling of business shares. Another law, outlawing child labour in factories everywhere, was declared to be illegal by the Supreme Court. Many people still distrusted too much government 'interference' in the nation's life.

The United States and the First World War

The First World War

In August 1914, what came to be known as the First World War began in Europe. One by one the major European countries were drawn into it. The main countries on one side were France, Britain and Russia, known as the Allies. On the other side the main countries were Germany and Austria, known as the Central Powers.

Most Americans wanted to keep out of the war. They saw it as a purely European affair that was not their concern. President Wilson advised them not to take sides. Here is part of a speech that he made in the first weeks of the war:

> 'The people of the United States are drawn from many nations, and chiefly from the nations now at war . . . [They] may be divided into camps of hostile opinion, hot against each other, involved in the war itself in . . . opinion if not in action.
>
> I venture, therefore, my fellow countrymen, to speak a solemn word of warning to you . . . The United States must be neutral in fact as well as in name during these days . . . We must be impartial in thought as well as in action.'
>
> President Woodrow Wilson, 18 August 1914.

Arms for the Allies

But Americans found it difficult to stay impartial for long. From the very beginning of the war, trade between the United States and the Allies grew quickly. By 1915 American factories were making vast

'American voters re-elected Wilson largely because he had kept them out of the war.' Election slogans in New Jersey, 1916.

quantities of weapons and munitions and selling them to Britain and France. German leaders were determined to stop this flow of armaments to their enemies. They announced in February 1915 that they would sink all Allied merchant ships in the seas around the British Isles.

The *Lusitania*, 1915

On a hazy afternoon in May 1915, a large British ship called the *Lusitania*, carrying both passengers and cargo, was nearing the end of its voyage from the United States to Britain. Suddenly, without any warning, it was hit by a torpedo from a German submarine. Within minutes the *Lusitania* was sinking. More than 1,000 passengers went with it to the bottom of the ocean. Of these, 128 were Americans.

A shock of horror swept across the United States. It was quickly followed by one of anger. Americans began to realise that their country might be drawn into this war whether it wanted to be or not. In January of the following year Congress voted the money needed to make the fighting forces ready for war.

Wilson for peace

Most Americans still wanted peace, however. President Wilson made strong protests to the German government about the *Lusitania* sinking and for a time the Germans stopped the submarine attacks. When American voters re-elected Wilson as President in the autumn of 1916 it was largely because he had kept them out of the war.

Moving towards war

But by now American bankers had lent vast amounts of money to the Allies. And American supplies for the British and French armies were still pouring across the Atlantic. Germany's war leaders feared that, unless the flow of supplies was stopped, their country would be defeated. In February 1917, they again ordered their submarines to begin sinking ships steaming for allied ports. This time the order included neutral vessels.

In the next few weeks German submarines sank five American ships. Wilson felt that he now had no choice. On 2 April 1917, he asked Congress to declare war on Germany.

Opposition to war

Several members of Congress spoke out against Wilson's request. One of them was Senator George W. Norris from the western farming state of Nebraska. This is part of what he said:

'I feel that we are committing a sin against humanity and against our countrymen . . . It seems to me that this war craze has robbed us of our judgment.

The troubles of Europe ought to be settled by Europe . . . We ought to remain absolutely neutral and permit them to settle their questions without our interference . . . Upon the passage of this resolution [to declare war] we will have joined Europe in the great catastrophe and taken America into entanglements that will not end with this war, but will live and bring their evil influences upon many generations yet unborn.'

Senator George W. Norris, April 1917.

Wilson's war aims

But Norris's arguments failed to convince his fellow members of Congress. On 6 April, 1917, after four days of debate, Congress voted for war.

Wilson's aim was not simply to defeat Germany. He saw the war as a great crusade to ensure the future peace of the world. For him it was a war 'to make the world safe for democracy, the war to end all wars'.

American troops land in France in 1917.

The Fourteen Points

Wilson always insisted that the United States was fighting the First World War not against the German people but against their war-like leaders. In January 1918, he outlined his ideas for a just and lasting peace in a speech to the United States Senate. These ideas were called the Fourteen Points.

Amongst other things, Wilson's Fourteen Points said that nations should stop making secret agreements, reduce their military forces and armaments, trade freely with one another and draw up new national boundaries that would allow the separate peoples of Europe to rule themselves. It was in the Fourteen Points, also, that Wilson first suggested setting up an international peace-keeping organisation called the League of Nations.

Making an army

When the United States declared war on Germany in April 1917, the American army consisted of only 200,000 soldiers. Millions more men had to be recruited, trained, equipped and shipped across the Atlantic to Europe. All this took time. A full year passed before many American soldiers were available to help the European Allies.

In the spring of 1918 the German armies began a last desperate offensive against the French and the British. Their aim was to win the war before the new American army was ready to fight. By July they were within a few miles of Paris.

The Allies were in great danger. But now American soldiers began to arrive at the front to strengthen the Allied forces. Soon over a million of them had joined in the battles against the Germans.

Germany defeated, 1918

In August 1918, the Allied armies counter-attacked and the German armies were driven back towards their own frontiers. In October the German government saw that the war was lost and asked for peace. On 11 November 1918, German and Allied leaders signed an armistice, an agreement to stop fighting. The bloodiest and most destructive war the world had ever known was over.

Making the peace

By January 1919, President Wilson was in Europe to help to work out a peace treaty. He was greeted by cheering crowds in the Allied capitals and spoken of as 'Wilson the Just'.

Allied leaders disagree

But when Wilson met other Allied leaders to work out the details of the treaty, his welcome became less friendly. When the German government asked for peace in October 1918, it had hoped that the Allies would base their terms on Wilson's Fourteen Points. But other Allied leaders regarded some of Wilson's ideas as idealistic nonsense. The French leader, Clemençeau, compared the Fourteen Points sarcastically to the Christian religion's Ten Commandments. 'Mr Wilson bores me with his Fourteen Points,' he grumbled. 'Why, God Almighty has only ten!'

Both Wilson and Clemençeau wanted to make sure that a war like the First World War never happened again. Wilson wanted to do this by writing a treaty that did not leave the Germans with lots of grievances. He believed that if the Germans thought they had not been treated fairly, they might one day start a war of revenge.

Clemençeau thought differently. He believed there was only one way to make a peace that would last. The Germans had to be made so weak that they would never have the strength to fight again.

The Versailles Treaty

After much arguing, and without consulting the defeated Germans, the Allied leaders finally agreed on a peace treaty. They called it the Versailles Treaty, after the palace near Paris where it was signed in May, 1919.

Wilson was disappointed with much of the Versailles Treaty. It was harder in its treatment of the Germans than he had wanted. Amongst other things it made them take all the blame for the war. It also made them agree to pay for all the damage that the war had caused. These 'reparation' payments were fixed at many millions of dollars.

But Wilson returned to the United States with high hopes for part of the Treaty. This was a scheme that he believed could still make his dream of a world without war come true. It was a plan to set up a League of Nations.

The League of Nations

The League of Nations was to be an organisation where representatives of the world's nations would meet and settle their differences by discussion instead of war. It had taken Wilson months of hard bargaining to persuade the other Allied leaders to accept this plan. Now he faced a battle to persuade Congress and the American people to accept it, too.

Americans and the League

Wilson knew that this would not be easy. Many Americans were against their country becoming permanently involved in the problems of Europe. They were especially suspicious of the League of Nations. Wouldn't joining such an organisation mean that the United States might be dragged into quarrels, perhaps even wars, that were none of its business? People who thought like this came to be called 'Isolationists'. This was because they believed that the United States should try to isolate itself from the quarrels of the outside world.

Isolationists

One of the main spokesmen for the Isolationist point of view was a Republican Senator from Massachusetts named Henry Cabot Lodge. Wilson had made an enemy of Lodge, and of other Republican leaders, by failing to consult them during the working out of the Versailles Treaty. Whilst Wilson was still in Europe, Lodge told an audience in Boston:

> 'Under Article Ten of this treaty we have got to take our army and our navy and go to war with any country which attempts aggression upon the territorial integrity of another member of the League.
>
> Now, that is a tremendous promise to make. I ask fathers and mothers, sisters, wives and sweethearts, whether they are ready . . . to send the hope of their families, the hope of the nation, the best of our youth . . . on that errand?'
> Senator Henry Cabot Lodge, Boston, 19 March 1919.

Wilson tried to remove such fears. So did his supporters, including Franklin Roosevelt. Although Roosevelt had doubts about some of the details of Wilson's plan, he was convinced that the President was right in his belief that setting up some kind of international organisation was the only certain way to ensure the future peace of the world. He campaigned vigorously to persuade people to accept Wilson's scheme:

> 'We must open our eyes and see that modern civilisation has become so complex and the lives of civilised men so interwoven with the lives

of other men in other countries, as to make it impossible to be in this world and not of it.'

Franklin D. Roosevelt, March 1919.

As the months passed, however, it began to seem that Wilson was losing his fight to persuade Congress and the American people to back the League. After another trip to Europe he returned to the United States tired and ill, but determined to make a last effort. Boarding a special train, he set out on a speaking tour which was to take him all over the western parts of the country to plead for the League.

The tour was never completed. The exhausted Wilson suffered a stroke and was taken back to Washington, his health broken for ever. For Wilson, the battle for the League was over. The question now was, could the fight be won without him?

By 1920 many Americans were weary of foreign entanglements and Congress voted against the USA joining the League of Nations.

Roosevelt for Vice-President

The Democratic Convention, 1920

In 1920 the National Convention of the Democratic Party met in San Francisco to choose their candidate for that year's Presidential election. With Wilson a helpless invalid, their choice fell upon James M. Cox, the progressive Governor of the state of Ohio. The next job was to choose a candidate for Vice-President. Much to his surprise the man the Convention picked was Franklin Roosevelt. When told of the choice, his first reaction was disbelief. 'Quit kidding me,' he said.

Why Roosevelt?

But it was true. Roosevelt had been chosen partly for his well known support for the ideas of Wilson, partly for his famous name and partly because he 'balanced the ticket' – that is, he came from a different part of the country from Cox and would therefore attract additional votes in the campaign. But he was chosen, too, because of the reputation as an able and hard-fighting politician which he had by now built up for himself and because of the efficient way in which he had carried out his duties as Assistant Secretary to the Navy during the war.

The League question

The most important decision Cox and Roosevelt had to make in planning their campaign was what to do about the League. It was becoming clearer than ever now that many people were opposed to the United States' entry. Yet Roosevelt still had faith in the idea and so to a lesser extent had Cox. What ought they to do?

Cox decided that they would give full support to the League. He and Roosevelt visited Wilson to tell him of their decision. They found the President sitting in an armchair on the White House porch.

Roosevelt was shocked by the change in Wilson's appearance. His face was pale and drawn and his eyes were dulled. Only once during their short interview did he seem to become fully alive. This was when Cox told him that he and Roosevelt intended to give full support to the League in their campaign. Wilson struggled to speak: 'Mr Cox,' he whispered at last, 'the fight can still be won!'

Harding and normalcy

He was wrong. It could not. Cox and Roosevelt put up a good fight, but the tide of public opinion was running against them. By 1920 many Americans were weary of talk about social reforms and the brotherhood of man. What they wanted was a chance to get back to living an ordinary uncomplicated life. This is what the Republican Presidential candidate, Warren Harding, promised them. He called it 'normalcy', a word which he made up himself. In November the American people elected Harding as their President by a large majority.

Rejecting the League

Harding's victory marked the end of the last hope of the United States joining the League of Nations. Congress had already voted against the idea and now it was dropped completely. From his invalid's armchair in the White House a sick and bitter Wilson spoke the last words upon the subject: 'We had a chance to gain the leadership of the world. We have lost it, and soon we shall be witnessing the tragedy of it all.'

5

The Roaring Twenties:
The Bright Side

Republicans and industry

Republicans rule

Throughout the 1920s the United States was ruled by a succession of Republican Presidents – first by Warren Harding (1921–23), then by Calvin Coolidge (1923–29) and finally by Herbert Hoover (1929–33). In Congress, too, the Republican party was strongly represented during these years.

The main reason for the popularity of the Republicans was that by the middle of the 1920s many Americans were better off than ever before. The Republicans claimed that much of the prosperity was the result of their policies.

Republican economic policies

Republican policies were based upon the simple belief that if the government helped businessmen to prosper, then everyone would be better off. A businessman whose firm was doing well would be able to employ more workers and to pay them higher wages. In this way a share of the increasing wealth of factory owners and investors would trickle down and benefit people at all levels of society.

So Republican governments set out to create the most favourable conditions they could for American business. They placed high tariffs, or import taxes, upon goods from abroad, so that manufacturers would not have to face foreign competition in selling their products. To give the rich more money to invest they reduced the taxes on high incomes and company profits that had been imposed during the war. Attempts such as those made by Theodore Roosevelt and Woodrow Wilson to limit the power of corporations and trusts were almost entirely given up. Why bother? If the growth of trusts caused industries to be run more efficiently, then let them grow. Businessmen became popular heroes. They were widely admired as the creators of the nation's prosperity. 'The man who builds a factory builds a temple,' said President Calvin Coolidge. 'The man who works there worships there.'

The motor industry

Such favourable government attitudes helped American industry to grow rapidly during the 1920s. Leading the way was the motor industry. In 1910, when Franklin Roosevelt used the Red Peril in his New

York Senate campaign, motor cars and trucks were still novelties to many people. By the 1920s this was no longer so. In 1920 there were already over nine million motor vehicles registered in the USA. By 1929 it was calculated that there were enough cars in the United States to have sent the whole population of the country speeding along the roads at the same time.

Henry Ford and mass production

The leading figure in the car-making industry was Henry Ford. The son of a farmer, Ford built his first car in a backyard shed in 1896. It was twelve years later, however, that he produced the car that was to make his fortune – the Model 'T', affectionately known to millions of Americans as the 'Tin Lizzie'.

The Tin Lizzie

The Model 'T' was neither pretty nor comfortable. But it was tough, it was reliable and it would go anywhere, even where there were no roads. Above all it was cheap, and as the years passed it became even cheaper. In 1909 a Model 'T' cost 950 dollars; by 1913, 600 dollars; by 1917, 360 dollars. As the price fell, sales increased. The Model 'T' became the most popular car in the world.

Henry Ford himself described the Model 'T' as 'the universal car'. Farmers could fit special wheels and use it as a tractor to plough their fields. They could jack up its back end and run the engine to generate electricity. True, it had some awkward habits. When it was going up-hill, for example, the petrol sometimes refused to flow through to the engine and everyone had to get out and push. A popular joke of the time said that with every car Ford supplied a monkey, to pick up the nuts that were likely to drop off it.

Henry Ford did not mind the jokes. Every joke sold a car, he said. By the time the Model 'T' finally stopped being made in 1927, over fifteen million had been sold, more than any other car either before or since.

Standardisation and mass production

The secret of the Tin Lizzie's cheapness was the fact that it was mass produced. As early as 1903 Ford said to a friend, 'The real way is to make one like another, as much alike as pins or matches.' When the friend said that this was impossible, Ford replied, 'The principle is just the same. All you need is more space.'

Ford tried out his idea with the Model 'T'. Every car was assembled from exactly the same parts. They were even painted the same colour. 'Any customer can have a car painted any colour that he wants,' Ford is supposed to have said, 'so long as it is black.'

The assembly line

A few years later Ford combined this idea of standardisation with that of the moving assembly line, which saved time by taking work to the workers instead of workers to the work.

Ford tried out the assembly line first on making magnetos. By the old method of magneto-making one man did the whole job from start to finish. Putting together a magneto in this way took twenty minutes. Ford split the job up into twenty-one separate actions. A different man carried out each one as the magneto moved past him on a 'conveyor' or moving belt. The result was that assembly time was cut to five minutes.

In 1913 Ford started using the assembly line method to make the complete Model 'T'. Before this, putting together a Model 'T' had taken 12 hours, 28 minutes. Splitting the job up into forty-five separate actions cut assembly time to 1 hour, 33 minutes. This is how Ford himself described the system in action:

> 'In the chassis assembly line are forty-five separate operations. The first men fasten four mudguard brackets to the chassis frame; the motor arrives on the tenth operation and so on. Some men do only one or two small operations, others do more. The man who places a part does not fasten it. The man who puts in a bolt does not put on the nut; the man who puts on the nut does not tighten it. On operation thirty-four the motor gets its gasolene; on operation forty-four the radiator is filled with water and on operation forty-five the car drives out into John R. Street.'
>
> Henry Ford, *My Life and Work*, 1922.

Consumer goods and credit

The industrial boom

The spectacular increase in motor manufacturing in the 1920s stimulated the growth of other American industries. Steel was needed for car and truck bodies and engines; glass for windscreens; leather for seats; rubber for tyres; and petrol (known as gasolene or gas to Americans) for power. The industries producing these things all benefited from the motor boom.

The consumer boom

In the 1920s the United States became the first nation in history to build its way of life on selling vast quantities of goods that gave ordinary people easier and more enjoyable lives. Not only cars, but other 'consumer goods' such as radios, cleaners and refrigerators, poured off the assembly lines of big new factories. Between 1919 and 1929 such mass-production factories doubled their output.

This rapid growth of industry made possible a remarkable rise in the American standard of living. Wages were higher, profits were higher. Many Americans had more money in their pockets than ever before.

Instalment plans

To help them to spend it, new shops began to appear on main streets all over America. Their more expensive goods could be bought by hire purchase, or 'on the instalment plan' as Americans described it. A small deposit now, a promise to pay the rest later, and anyone could have that new washer, refrigerator or car that they had been longing for. True, you were spending next year's income before you had earned

Mass production. Model Ts reach the end of the Ford assembly line in Detroit, 1913.

it, but why worry? It seemed that the more everyone spent the faster the wheels of industry went round and the better off everyone was.

Radio

One of the most common instalment plan 'buys' was a radio set. The first commercial broadcasting station crackled on to the air in Pittsburgh in 1920. Within a few years stations had opened up all over the country, and radio receivers in elaborately-carved wooden cabinets were bringing entertainment and information right into American living rooms. By 1929 the United States had nine million homes with radios in them and radio manufacturing had become an important new industry employing many people.

The younger generation

After the anxieties of the war years people were eager to enjoy themselves in the 1920s. This was especially true of the young. Many began to rebel against the rules of behaviour laid down for them by their elders. For the first time girls from respectable homes began to wear make-up. Their skirts grew shorter, inching their way up from the ankles to the knees by the end of the 1920s. Older people shook their heads and wondered what the younger generation was coming to.

Hollywood and the movies

In the 1920s both young and old were passionate fans of the motion pictures, or 'movies'. Since the early years of the century, motion picture theatres, or cinemas, had opened in most American towns, and by the end of the 1920s Americans were buying a hundred million cinema tickets every week. 'Going to the movies' had become a national habit.

Hollywood

Most American films were made in Hollywood, a suburb of the Californian city of Los Angeles. Hollywood's big attraction for film-makers was its clean air and plentiful sunshine, which meant that the movies made there were bright and clear. By the 1920s it had become the film-making capital of the world. Because the movies of the 1920s were silent and told their stories in pictures, not in words, their language was international.

Movie making at a Hollywood studio, 1928.

Studios and standardisation

Hollywood movies were made by large companies called studios. The men who ran them wanted to make as much money as possible. They soon found that one way to do this was to 'standardise' their films in the same way that Henry Ford had standardised his cars. Once audiences had shown that they liked a certain kind of film, the Hollywood studios made many more of exactly the same kind.

The star system

Another sure way to make money out of movies was for a studio to turn its actors into 'stars'. Stars were actors who were so popular that people flocked to see any film they appeared in. A famous star, like the wide-eyed heroine Mary Pickford or the romantic hero Rudolph Valentino, could make any film a certain success.

Charlie Chaplin

The most famous star of the 1920s was a little tramp with big boots, baggy trousers and a tooth-brush moustache. He was the first film star to become world famous. Soldiers sang about him as they marched into battle. Children chanted his name in their skipping rhymes. His name was Charlie Chaplin.

Chaplin was born in London in 1889 and in the 1890s he became a boy actor. He soon found that he was especially good at mime. By the early 1900s he had become a popular music-hall turn. His favourite part was that of a drunk. With a bowler hat perched on the side of his head, he would wander on to the stage and start interfering in the performance. He would argue with the actors, get in the way of the stage-hands, insult the musicians. The audience loved it.

Chaplin in Hollywood

In 1913 Charlie Chaplin went to the United States. There he decided to try his luck in Hollywood. One day he borrowed an outsize pair of trousers, a tight coat and a pair of boots that were much too big, and set off with a camera man for a nearby fairground. The comic film he made there was a great success. His little tramp had been born and became so popular with movie goers that rival studios gave Chaplin more and more money to make films for them. Between 1914 and 1916 his income rose from 150 dollars to 10,000 dollars a week.

Chaplin's success

The secret of Chaplin's success was his skill as a screen actor. He knew that the film camera could pick up the tiniest gesture and magnify it many times. So he made every movement count. The lift of an eyebrow, the flick of a finger – every movement told the audience something about the little man and the way he was feeling.

In his later films Chaplin sometimes laid aside the bowler hat and the baggy trousers of the little tramp. The films often dealt in a humorous way with serious problems, like the stresses of working on the production lines of a modern factory (*Modern Times*, 1936) or the threat of dictators like Hitler (*The Great Dictator*, 1940).

But even in these later years, when most people heard the name Charlie Chaplin they still thought of the cheeky little tramp whose image flickered across cinema screens all over the world during the 1920s.

6

The Roaring Twenties: The Dark Side

Roosevelt's fight against polio

Out of politics

When Warren Harding moved into the White House as President in the spring of 1921 he brought his own followers to Washington to take over the running of the government. For the first time in ten years Franklin Roosevelt found himself without a job in politics.

He was not altogether sorry. His years in the Navy Department had taught him a lot – how to run a large and complicated government department, for instance, and how to divide up his time in order to deal with a heavy load of work. He was ready for a change, though, and together with two friends he set up as a lawyer once more.

Polio strikes

Early in August, 1921, Roosevelt went to join his wife and their five children on a holiday by the sea in New England. Shortly after his arrival the whole family went out for a sail. On the way home they spotted a forest fire and went ashore to beat it out. It was hot and dirty work, and when they arrived back at their holiday cottage they all dived into a nearby lake to cool down and wash off the dirt.

The next morning Roosevelt felt feverish and ached all over. By the following day he found that he was losing the use of his legs. It was clear that something was seriously wrong, and a medical specialist was sent for. His examination confirmed what Roosevelt already feared; he had been attacked by polio.

In 1921 polio was a disease about which little was known. A bad attack often killed its victim, and those who survived were usually left crippled for life. For weeks Roosevelt lay close to death, tortured by pain and with much of his body paralysed.

Fighting back

But Roosevelt fought grimly to hold on to life. By the end of October 1921, he was showing slight signs of improvement. Slowly, painfully, he regained the use of his back and arm muscles. A gymnasium ring hung from the ceiling of his room enabling him to pull himself up by his arms and turn in bed. After months of lying completely helpless, the ability to move by his own efforts seemed a great achievement and Roosevelt became more cheerful.

Next he learned how to sit up and to move about his room in a wheel chair. Then came the most cheering advance of all. Early in 1922 his doctor fitted him with steel braces, lengths of tubing which were strapped to his legs and locked rigidly into position. Wearing these, and with the aid of a pair of crutches, Roosevelt found that he could stand upright and even walk after a fashion.

Back at work

Soon he was managing to get to work again, travelling to his office by car and staying at his desk once he arrived there. He showed no sign of self pity for his crippled condition. He told a friend:

> 'I can't move around my office, but what advantage is there in moving around an office anyhow? I used to walk the rug in the old days, and what did I accomplish? I wore a hole in the rug. I thought I was thinking but I was just walking, just walking, that's all.'
>
> Franklin Roosevelt in 1922, quoted in R. Harrity and R. G. Martin, *The Human Side of F.D.R.*, 1960.

'He grew bigger'

When Franklin Roosevelt was President of the United States, years after his polio attack, a friend named Louis Howe spoke about the attack's effects upon him:

> 'There are times when I think that Franklin might never have been President if he had not been stricken. You see, he had a thousand interests. He rode, he swam, he played golf, tennis, he sailed, he collected stamps, he politicked, he did every damned thing under the sun a man could think of doing. Then suddenly there he was flat on his back with nothing to do but think. He began to read, he began to think, he talked, he gathered people around him – his thoughts expanded, his horizon widened. He began to see the other fellow's point of view. He thought of others who were ill and afflicted and in want. He dwelt on many things that had not bothered him much before. Lying there, he grew bigger, day by day.'
>
> Louis Howe, quoted in *The Human Side of F.D.R.*

Eleanor Roosevelt, too, referred in later years to the effects of the illness on her husband's character. It gave him, she said, 'strength and courage he had not had before. He had to learn the greatest of all lessons – infinite patience and never-ending persistence.' His illness taught Franklin Roosevelt other things, too, including a confident, optimistic attitude to problems of all kinds. The fact that he had beaten death made him believe he could beat anything. As one of his advisers put it, 'The guy never knows when he is licked.'

His confidence was catching. Someone who saw him with other polio sufferers described the cheering effect that his presence had upon them: 'He was one of them – he was a big brother – he had been through it – he was smiling – he was courageous – he was feeling fine – he encouraged you to try – he said you could do it.'

Roosevelt's ability to give other people confidence became one of the secrets of his success as a political leader. The fight against polio also helped his political career in another way. Previously his wealthy background had made many people think that although he might sympathise with the problems of ordinary people, he could never really understand them. How could he? What suffering or hardship had he ever known?

After his illness people saw Roosevelt differently. They saw a man who had faced up to terrible misfortune and fought against it courageously and successfully. He was no longer an outsider; he was one of them.

Prohibition and the bootleggers

Prohibition

In 1919 the American people voted in favour of a change, or amendment, to the Constitution of the United States. This Eighteenth Amendment prohibited the making or selling of alcoholic drinks in the United States. People who supported Prohibition (they were nicknamed 'dries') claimed that by stopping drunkenness it would make people healthier and happier.

Bootleggers

But many Americans were not willing to give up alcohol. Millions of these 'wets' began to break the prohibition law deliberately and regularly. Illegal drinking places called 'speakeasies' opened in basements and backrooms all over the country. The city of Chicago had 10,000 of them. New York had 32,000.

Speakeasies obtained their 'booze' from criminals called 'bootleggers', who worked together in gangs called 'mobs'. The best known mob was one in Chicago led by the gangster 'Scarface' Al Capone.

Bootlegging was a dangerous business. Competition between rival gangs sometimes caused bloody street wars, fought out with armoured cars and machine guns. The winners of the gangster wars became rich and powerful. They used their wealth to bribe police and other public officials to do nothing about their law-breaking.

Al Capone

Al Capone became the real ruler of Chicago. He had a private army of nearly a thousand machine-gun-equipped thugs and his income was over 100 million dollars a year. Capone claimed that he was just another American businessman, working hard to supply the needs of his customers. This is how he defended his behaviour to reporters:

'I'm a businessman. I've made my money by supplying a popular demand. If I break the law my customers are as guilty as I am. When I sell liquor it's bootlegging. When my patrons serve it on silver trays it's hospitality. The country wanted booze and I've organized it. Why should I be called a public enemy?

When Prohibition came in there were 7,500 saloons in Chicago.

Nobody wanted Prohibition. This town voted six to one against it. Somebody had to throw some liquor on that thirst. Why not me? My customers include some of the finest people in the city, or in the world for that matter, but I'm just a bootlegger. I violate the Prohibition law. All right, so do they.'

Al Capone in 1929, quoted in Kenneth Allsop, *The Bootleggers*, 1961.

The St Valentine's Day Massacre, Chicago, 1929. Seven gangsters lie dead, shot by rival bootleggers.

The effects of prohibition

By the end of the 1920s most Americans regarded Prohibition as half-scandal, half-joke. The dishonesty and corruption which grew with it made them lose their respect both for the law and for the people who were supposed to enforce it.

Prohibition was finally given up in 1933. But by then it had done the United States lasting harm. It made law-breaking a habit for many otherwise respectable Americans. And gangsters remained powerful. Many used the money they had made as bootleggers to set up other criminal businesses.

Immigrants not wanted

The flood of immigrants into the United States in the early years of the twentieth century – more than thirteen million of them in its first fifteen years – worried many Americans. Most of the immigrants were from south-east Europe. They were poor, unskilled and unable to speak English.

Americans born in the United States felt threatened by the newcomers. They accused them of taking jobs away from American-born workers; of lowering standards of health and education; of threatening the country's traditions and way of life by bringing in 'un-American' political ideas like anarchism and communism.

The Immigration Restriction League

An organisation called the Immigration Restriction League gave what it claimed was scientific support to such prejudices. It said that the new immigrants were racially inferior. The future of the United States, it asserted, depended upon its people being bred from only the best human stock. A document issued by the League in 1910 said this:

> 'We should exercise at least as much care in admitting human beings as we exercise in relation to animals or insect pests or disease germs. Yet . . . we are today taking actually more care in the selection . . . of a Hereford bull or a Southdown ewe . . . than we are taking in the selection of the alien men and women who are coming here to be the fathers and mothers of future American children . . . .
>
> A considerable proportion of immigrants now coming are from races and countries . . . which have not progressed, but which have been backward, downtrodden and relatively useless for centuries . . . There is no reason to suppose that a change of location will result in a change of inborn tendencies.'
>
> Immigration Restriction League pamphlet, quoted in
> Maldwyn A. Jones, *Destination America*, 1976.

Ku Klux Klan

Another group that was particularly hostile towards immigrants was an organisation called the Ku Klux Klan. The Klan dated back to the years after the American Civil War of the 1860s. It had been formed originally to maintain white supremacy in the American south by threatening and terrorising black people to prevent them from claiming their rights.

In the 1920s the Ku Klux Klan took on a new lease of life. It claimed that its aim was to 'maintain the traditions and ideals of pure Americanism', but in fact it spent its time in stirring up religious and racial hatred. Hiding their identities behind pointed white hoods, its members preached the supremacy of white people over Negroes, of Christians over Jews, and of Protestants over Catholics.

The Klan's methods were to threaten, to torture, and even to murder its victims. A magazine reported these examples of its activities in the state of Alabama in the mid-1920s:

'A lad whipped with branches until his back was ribboned flesh; a Negress beaten and left helpless to contract pneumonia from exposure and die; a white girl, divorcée, beaten into unconsciousness in her own home; a naturalized foreigner flogged until his back was a pulp because he married an American woman; a Negro lashed until he sold his land to a white man for a fraction of its value.'

R. A. Patton in *Current History*, quoted in F. L. Allen, *Only Yesterday*, 1931.

By 1925 the Ku Klux Klan had five million members and was powerful enough in some states – Oklahoma, Oregon and Indiana, for example – to exert great influence over their governments.

'The Klan spent its time in stirring up religious and racial hatred.' Swearing in new recruits to the Ku Klux Klan in the 1920s.

The 'Red Scare'

In 1917 a communist revolution had taken place in Russia. These early Russian communists believed that all property should be controlled by the government on behalf of the community. They called upon workers in other countries to rise in revolution.

By 1919 some Americans feared that communist revolutionaries, or 'reds', were plotting a take-over in the United States. A 'Red Scare' began. People who criticised the way American society was organised risked being labelled as traitors. This risk was especially great for anyone who supported socialist ideas. Such ideas were thought to be 'un-American', and people who held them were feared and persecuted, especially if they were foreign-born.

An early twentieth century anti-immigrant cartoon. European rulers dance with joy as emigrant 'rats' are attracted to the United States. The 'Black Hand' was a pre-1914 European terrorist group.

In January, 1920, the Federal government arrested over 6,000 suspected communists. Very few of those arrested had done anything illegal and most were soon released. But 550 who had been born abroad were deported.

Sacco and Vanzetti

On 15 April 1920, two people were shot dead in a $15,000 robbery near Boston. Witnesses said that two of the robbers looked 'very Italian'. Three weeks later two Italian immigrants named Nicola Sacco and Bartolomeo Vanzetti were arrested.

Both had alibis for the time of the murder. But Sacco owned a gun that could have been used in the killings. Both men were dark skinned and looked Italian. And both were foreigners who held left-wing political ideas.

The judge at their trial disliked all these things. He told friends that he was going to 'get those anarchist bastards', and eventually sentenced both Sacco and Vanzetti to death. Many believed that he had condemned the two men for their origins and political beliefs, not because of the evidence against them. For six years people both in the United States and abroad fought for their release. On 27 May 1927, however, both were executed.

Vanzetti's last statement

Sacco and Vanzetti protested to the end that they were innocent. When told that he was to be executed, Vanzetti said this:

> 'I not only am not guilty of these crimes, but I never commit a crime in my life. I have never steal and I have never kill and I have never spilt blood. I have suffered for things that I am guilty of. I am suffering because I am a radical and indeed I am a radical. I have suffered because I am an Italian and indeed I am an Italian. But I am so convinced to be right that if you could execute me two times, and if I could be reborn two other times, I would live again to do what I have done already.'
>
> Bartolomeo Vanzetti, April 1927, quoted in Hugh Brogan, *Longman History of the United States*, 1985.

To this day neither the guilt nor the innocence of Sacco and Vanzetti has been finally proved. But their case is remembered as an example of how justice may suffer when attitudes are affected by prejudice.

The Immigration Act, 1924

By the time Sacco and Vanzetti went to their deaths Congress had passed laws to limit all kinds of immigration. The one which had most effect was the Reed-Johnson Immigration Act of 1924.

The 1924 Immigration Act reflected the fears and the prejudices of Americans who were descendants of earlier north European immigrants. It said that in future no more than 150,000 immigrants a year would be let into the United States. Each country which sent immigrants was given a 'quota'. The quota was based on the number of its people already living in the United States. The more it had there already, the more new immigrants it would be allowed to send.

The Immigration Act's effects

The 1924 system was designed to reduce immigration from southern and eastern Europe. And it worked. Once it began to operate, 87 per cent of the immigration permits that were granted went to immigrants from Britain, Ireland, Germany and Scandinavia – the countries from which the ancestors of most 1920s Americans had originally come.

Hard times for workers and farmers

Hoover promises prosperity

In the summer of 1928, a few months before American voters elected him to be the next President of the United States, Herbert Hoover made this confident statement:

> 'We in America today are nearer to the final triumph over poverty than ever before in the history of our land. The poor man is vanishing from among us. Under ... the Republican protective system, our industrial output has increased as never before, and our wages have grown steadily in buying power. Our workers with their average weekly wages can today buy two or even three times more bread and butter than any wage earner in Europe.'
>
> Herbert Hoover, summer, 1928.

Poor Americans

Yet there were still lots of poor Americans when Hoover spoke. A survey in the following year showed that half the American people had hardly enough money to buy sufficient food and clothing. In the industrial cities of the north, such as Chicago and Pittsburgh, immigrant workers still laboured long hours for low wages in steel mills, factories and slaughter houses. In the south thousands of poor farmers, some black and some white, worked from sunrise to sunset to earn barely enough to live on. The wealth that Republicans said would benefit everybody never reached people like these.

Farmers' problems

The main reason for poverty among industrial workers was low wages. Farmers and farm workers had a hard time for different reasons. In the south many farmers did not own the land they farmed. They were sharecroppers. For rent a sharecropper gave the landowner part of what he grew – often so much that he was left with hardly enough to feed his family.

In the west most farmers owned their land. But they, too, faced hard times. During the First World War they had been able to sell their wheat to Europe, but by 1921 the countries of Europe no longer needed it so much. Farmers were also finding it more difficult to sell their produce at home. Immigration had fallen, so the number of people needing food was growing more slowly. All the new cars pouring off Henry Ford's assembly lines didn't help either. Cars ran on petrol, not on corn and hay like horses.

American farmers found themselves growing products they could not sell. By 1924, 600,000 of them were bankrupt.

Hoover tries to help

Members of Congress from farming areas persuaded the Federal government to try to help. Hoover's government made it easier for farmers to borrow money. A Farm Board was set up which used government money to buy crops like wheat and cotton, which the farmers could not otherwise have sold.

But despite these efforts to help them, farmers found it more and more difficult to make ends meet. As American industry climbed steadily to ever higher peaks of prosperity, farming slid with increasing speed into a state of depression.

PART TWO

THE DEPRESSION AND THE NEW DEAL

7

Roosevelt Comes Back, Wall Street Crashes

Roosevelt comes back

It was 24 June 1924. At Madison Square Gardens, a great indoor arena in New York city, the National Convention of the Democratic Party was meeting to choose the party's candidate for that year's Presidential election.

Franklin Roosevelt sat in his wheelchair near the centre of the packed hall. He would soon be addressing a large crowd for the first time since his illness, for in a few moments he was due to make a speech in support of Al Smith, New York's candidate for the nomination.

Al Smith

Al Smith was the Governor of New York State and in this position he had brought about valuable reforms in such matters as housing and factory working conditions. Roosevelt had watched his career with admiration. Such a man would, he believed, make a good President. He had willingly agreed, therefore, to give Smith his help to become the Democratic party's candidate for the Presidency.

The 'happy warrior' speech

At last the moment came. Roosevelt's son Jimmy helped him to his crutches and locked the catch on his leg-braces into position, then together they walked slowly up the centre aisle to the speaker's platform. Here is how an eye witness described the scene:

'To those of us who remembered the strong, successful Roosevelt of the San Francisco convention of 1920, the man who appeared at Madison Square Gardens in 1924 was deeply moving. He was thin and pale. He struggled across the platform on crutches, smiling only when he reached the security of the speaker's rostrum. When he smiled at last, his face had a warm friendliness that included everyone in the auditorium. He seemed to be sharing his personal victory.'

Frances Perkins, *The Roosevelt I Knew*, 1946.

Roosevelt's speech in support of Smith was rated as one of the finest of the Convention. As he ended it by describing Smith as 'the happy

During the 1924 Presidential campaign, Roosevelt is visited at Hyde Park by Al Smith (far right).

warrior' a roar of applause rose from the crowd. It was as much in tribute to the crippled but gallant Roosevelt himself as to Smith.

Despite the enthusiasm which greeted Roosevelt's speech, Smith did not get the Democratic nomination. It went instead to an ex-Ambassador to Great Britain named John W. Davis. In the Presidential election later in the year Davis was heavily defeated by the Republican candidate, Calvin Coolidge.

Reforming the Democrats

The crushing defeat of Davis in the 1924 election convinced Roosevelt that the Democratic party must reform and modernise itself if it was to stand any chance of defeating the triumphant Republicans. Over the next few years he worked with other party leaders to bring about greater unity between Democrats in the industrial cities of the north and those in the rural areas of the south. Most important of all, he called for the party to present itself clearly to the people as a party of reform, which was determined to improve conditions of life for the ordinary person.

Roosevelt for New York State Governor

In 1928 Franklin Roosevelt again proposed to the Democratic National Convention that Al Smith should be the party's Presidential candidate.

This time Smith was accepted and Roosevelt again agreed to give him all the help he could in his election campaign.

Smith's Presidential campaign, 1928

It soon became clear that Smith wanted help in a way that Roosevelt had not expected. Now that he was running for President, Smith would not be able to offer himself for re-election as Governor of New York State, and the New York Democrats were afraid that they would lose the Governorship to the Republicans. To avoid this they wanted the strongest possible candidate to put in Smith's place. Who better, thought many of them, than a man of such proven ability and loyalty to the party as Franklin Roosevelt?

Reluctant candidate for Governor

Roosevelt was not keen on the idea. The Governorship of New York was a big job, which would leave him little time to continue treatment to improve the condition of his paralysed legs. There was another drawback, too. Roosevelt was pessimistic about the Democratic party's chances in the coming elections. Why should he risk probable defeat by returning to the political battlefield too soon?

When he was first approached to run for Governor, therefore, Roosevelt refused. But the appeals went on. Finally, Smith telephoned to ask him what he would do if the party ignored his refusal and insisted on choosing him nevertheless? Would he still refuse to run?

Roosevelt hesitated. To continue to refuse to run in those circumstances would mean that he might be accused of putting his personal interests before the good of the party.

Smith sensed his uncertainty. 'Thanks, Frank,' he shouted, and slammed down the telephone. The next day Roosevelt was nominated by a cheering New York State Convention as the Democratic candidate for the Governorship.

The campaign for Governor, 1928

When people heard that Roosevelt was a candidate for Governor many expressed anxiety about his health. Would he be able to stand the strain of the job? When Al Smith was asked this he answered dryly, 'We don't elect a governor for his ability to do a double back flip.'

Roosevelt himself gave his answer in actions instead of words. He threw himself into a whirlwind election tour which took him by train and by car to every corner of New York State. He made as many as seven major speeches in a day, his energy and enthusiasm never flagging. 'Too bad about this unfortunate sick man, isn't it?' he asked one audience, beaming cheerfully as he said it. To his family he remarked, 'If I could campaign another six months I could throw away my canes.'

Smith loses

At last the campaign was over. The voting for both the Presidency and the Governorship took place on the same day. The results of the voting in the Presidential election came in first. It soon became clear that Smith had been heavily defeated by the Republican candidate, Herbert Hoover. Even in Smith's home territory of New York Hoover had won.

The contest for the Governorship was closer, but by midnight the Republicans were ahead and looked like winning this, too. The atmosphere in Roosevelt's campaign headquarters was gloomy. Many of his supporters went wearily home, convinced that he had lost.

Roosevelt wins

Then, at about 2 a.m., there was a small stir of excitement. The radio announced that Roosevelt was winning unexpected votes in outlying areas of the state. Forty votes here, a hundred there, seventy-five somewhere else – his total crept upward. By 4 a.m. it was over. By a tiny majority Roosevelt had been elected Governor of New York State.

The Wall Street Boom

Wall Street

In the heart of New York city lies a narrow street enclosed by the walls of high office buildings. This is Wall Street, the nerve centre of American big business. Here can be found the New York Stock Exchange, where dealers called stockbrokers buy and sell share certificates. Each share certificate represents so much money invested in a business.

Hoover's confidence

In the spring of 1929 the stockbrokers of Wall Street were full of confidence. The new Republican President, Herbert Hoover, had just taken office. In his election campaign Hoover had made it clear that he intended to continue to encourage businessmen to run their affairs without interference from the government. If this were done, Hoover had claimed, American prosperity would go on increasing until there was 'a chicken in every pot and two cars in every garage'.

American prosperity

It was an attractive and believable picture. The prosperity of the United States was already the envy of the world. Its people earned higher wages than those of any other country. They owned more cars, more radios, more telephones. What was to stop this prosperity from growing? Weren't American factories the most up-to-date and efficient in the world? Weren't American resources of coal, iron, oil and almost every kind of raw material practically unlimited? And weren't American businessmen the cleverest the world had ever known?

Early in 1929 a leading businessman told Americans that they were 'only at the beginning of a period which will go down in history as a golden age'. To those who had invested money in businesses of one kind or another earlier in the 1920s, the 'golden age' seemed to have arrived already. They had seen the value of their investments rise steadily, for as the sales of goods like cars and radios increased so had the profits of the firms manufacturing them.

'Playing the market'

In order to share in these growing profits more and more people became eager to invest in leading industrial companies. By 1929 buying and selling shares on the Stock Exchange – 'playing the market', as it was called – had become almost a national pastime in America. Like radios, cars and most other purchases in the 1920s, shares could be brought on credit. A hundred dollars in cash would 'buy' a thousand dollars' worth of shares from any stockbroker. Many people borrowed large amounts of money from banks to buy shares in this way – 'on the margin', as it was called. Most 'on the margin' buyers were really gamblers. They bought shares with the intention of reselling them quickly at the increased price which they were sure the shares would reach in a few days.

The Wall Street Crash

Buy, buy, buy!

By the autumn of 1929 the urge to buy shares had become a sort of fever. Fantastic scenes took place in the New York Stock Exchange as dealers scrambled to buy the shares they wanted. One visitor wrote that the scene reminded him of a street fight.

Yet even while the fever to buy was at its height, some people began to have doubts. The true value of shares in a business firm depends upon its profits, and by the autumn of 1929 the profits being made by many firms had been falling for some time.

Sell, sell, sell!

If profits were falling, thought more cautious investors, then share prices, too, would soon fall. Slowly, such people began to sell their shares before this could happen. Day by day their numbers grew. Soon more people were selling shares than were buying them, and prices began to fall.

'The nerve centre of American big business.' Anxious crowds throng Wall Street after the stock market crash in October, 1929.

The Wall Street Crash

At first many investors held on to their shares, hoping that prices would begin to rise again. Instead the fall gathered speed. A panic began. Investors who earlier had clamoured to buy, now became even more eager to sell. By the end of October thousands found that shares for which they had paid high prices a few weeks earlier were now almost worthless. Many investors were ruined.

This collapse of share prices was known as the Wall Street Crash. It marked the end of the prosperous 1920s.

Causes of the Crash

'What had gone wrong?' people asked. Some blamed the blindness of politicians for the Crash, others the greed of investors and stockbrokers. But the Wall Street Crash had a more important cause. The fact was that by the end of the 1920s not enough people were buying the products of America's expanded industries. Why? Because too little of the USA's wealth was finding its way into the hands of the country's workers and farmers.

The most important cause of the Wall Street Crash was simply this – that too many Americans were not earning enough money to buy the goods that they themselves were producing.

The Depression begins

The Crash's effects: at home and abroad

The Wall Street Crash made people uncertain about the future. Many decided to save any money they had instead of spending it on new cars, radios, or other consumer goods. American factories were already making more goods than they could sell. Now they became even more short of customers.

The Crash affected sales to foreign countries, too. In the 1920s American goods had sold well overseas, especially in Europe. But countries such as Britain and Germany had not prospered after the war as the United States had. They had often paid for their purchases, and for the re-building of the war damaged industries of their countries, with money borrowed from American banks.

The Dawes Plan, 1924

The best known example of how this borrowing worked was a 1924 scheme called the Dawes Plan, named after the American banker who worked it out. Under the Dawes Plan, the United States lent money to Germany so that the Germans could pay reparations (see page 00) to France and the other Allies. The Allies were then able to use the reparation payments to start repaying their own wartime debts to the United States and to buy American goods.

The Hawley Smoot Tariff, 1931

After the Wall Street Crash, however, American banks wanted their money back. European buyers and manufacturers became short of cash. The situation became worse still when Congress passed the Hawley Smoot Act of 1931, which raised the already high American tariffs to the highest levels in the nation's history. The new law made it practically impossible for other nations to pay for American goods by selling their own products to the United States.

American overseas sales dried up almost completely. All over the United States, and throughout the rest of the industrialised world, goods piled up unsold in factory warehouses. Employers everywhere laid off workers and cut back production.

The unemployed

By the end of 1931 nearly eight million Americans were out of work. Unlike the millions of unemployed workers in countries such as Germany and Britain, they received no government unemployment pay. Many were soon without food and spent hours shuffling forward in queues called 'breadlines'. Here they received free pieces of bread or bowls of soup, paid for by money collected from those who could afford it.

By 1932 the position was worse still. Thousands of banks and over 100,000 businesses had closed down. Industrial production had fallen by half and wage payments by 60 per cent. New investment in industry

'Breadlines become everyday sights in American cities.' Unemployed New Yorkers queue in Times Square to receive free soup provided by one of the big newspapers.

was down by 90 per cent. Twelve million people, one out of every four of the country's workers, were unemployed. The city of Chicago alone had almost three quarters of a million workers without jobs. This was four out of ten of its normal working population.

The homeless

Many of the unemployed found themselves without homes, as well as without jobs. This is how one of them described a typical day in his life:

> 'You get shoved out early; you get your coffee and start walking. A couple of hours before noon you get in line. You eat and start walking. At night you sleep where you can. You don't talk. You eat what you can. You walk. No one talks to you. You walk. It's cold, and you shiver and stand in doorways or sit in railroad stations. You don't see much. You forget. You walk an hour and forget where you started from. It is day, and then it's night, and then it's day again. And you don't remember which was first. You walk.'
>
> M. Shulimson, *New Masses* magazine, January 1934.

The farmers

The Depression was easiest to see in the towns, with their silent factories, closed shops and slowly moving breadlines. But it brought ruin and despair to the farmlands also. Farmers simply could not sell their produce. With the number of people out of work rising day by day, their customers in the cities could no longer afford to buy. If anyone did buy, it was at the lowest possible prices. The same was true of the farmers' overseas customers.

Many farmers grew desperate. They took out shotguns and banded together to drive away men who came to throw them off their farms for not paying their debts. How can we pay, the farmers asked, when nobody will give us a fair price for our crops? They paraded through the streets in angry processions. They waved placards with words such as 'In Hoover we trusted, now we are busted.'

8

Hoover, Roosevelt and the Depression

President Hoover and the Depression

Brother, can you spare a dime?

One day in the early 1930s a young man in his twenties stood before a microphone in an American recording studio. At a signal from the recording engineer, an accompanying group played a short introduction and the singer began. His song told the story of a young man, a veteran of the First World War, begging for money from a passer-by. Here are some of its words:

> They used to tell me I was building a dream
> With peace and glory ahead –
> Why should I be standing in line
> Just waiting for bread?
>
> Once I built a railroad, made it run,
> Made it race against time.
> Once I built a railroad,
> Now it's done –
> Brother, can you spare a dime?
>
> Once in khaki suits,
> Gee, we looked swell,
> Full of that Yankee Doodle-de-dum.
> Half a million boots went sloggin' thru Hell,
> I was the kid with the drum.

Then, when the singer reached the closing lines of the lyric, he made his voice break with emotion as he sang:

> Gee, don't you remember – they called me 'Al',
> It was 'Al' all the time.
> Gee, don't you remember I'm your pal!
> Buddy – can you spare a dime?

Song: 'Brother, can you spare a dime?',
by Gorney and Harburg, 1932.

This recording became a hit, both in the United States and in other countries. It helped to make the young man – his name was Bing Crosby – one of the world's most famous singers of popular songs.

The main reason for the success of 'Brother, can you spare a dime?' was that it reflected so well the problems that faced millions of Americans in the early 1930s. Every week found more of them without jobs, without houses, without food, without sufficient clothing.

Hoover's policies

By now people from every section of the community – industrial workers, farmers, office workers, businessmen – were calling upon President Hoover to take government action to deal with the Depression.

At first Hoover was reluctant to do this. The answer to the hardships of the Depression, he believed, was for individual Americans to help

Desperate for work, a man in Detroit advertises on the street.

themselves and one another. So he appealed to businessmen not to cut wages or to sack their employees. He asked people to give generously to the charities feeding the unemployed.

Only when it became clear that such voluntary measures were not enough did Hoover turn to government action. In 1932, at his suggestion, Congress set up an organisation called the Reconstruction Finance Corporation and voted it almost four million dollars of government money to help banks and other businesses. Congress also voted money for the President to spend on projects such as road and dam building schemes. The idea was that by creating jobs such schemes would help to end the Depression by putting money back into the economy. By the time Hoover's Presidency came to an end early in 1933 the Federal government was spending five hundred million dollars a year more on public works than it had done in 1928.

Balancing the budget

However, Hoover insisted that he would only set up such schemes if his government had enough cash coming in from taxes to pay for them. He turned down the advice of some experts that he should borrow money to pay for job-creating schemes. This was because he believed that one of his first duties as the nation's President was to 'balance the budget' – that is, to make sure that the government's spending did not exceed the income that it received from taxation.

Restoring confidence

Hoover's main tactic in dealing with the Depression was to try to convince Americans that the economic situation was improving. If only he could restore people's confidence in the future, he believed, customers would start buying again, businessmen would start taking on workers and the nation would soon be on its way to recovery.

So time and time again in the early 1930s Hoover claimed that recovery from the Depression was 'just around the corner'. In a typical speech in May 1930, he told the American people 'We have now passed the worst and with continued unity of effort we shall recover.'

Hard times continue

But factories continued to close. Breadlines grew longer. People became hungrier. In 1931 a local midwife wrote this song about people's lives in the coal mining district of Harlan County in the state of Kentucky:

> The minin' town I live in
>   is a sad an' a lonely place,
> For pity and starvation
>   is pictured on every face,
> Everybody hungry and ragged,
>   no slippers on their feet,
> All goin' round from place to place
>   bummin' for a little food to eat.
>
> Song by Aunt Molly Jackson, 1931.

The 'bonus army'

In the spring of 1932 thousands of unemployed ex-servicemen poured into Washington, the nation's capital. They wanted the government to hand over some bonus payments that it owed them from the war years. The newspapers called them the 'bonus army'.

The men of the bonus army were determined to stay in Washington until the President did something to help them. On the edge of the city, at a place called Anacostia Flats, they set up a camp of rough shelters and huts. Similar camps could be found on rubbish dumps outside every large American city by this time. The homeless people who lived in them named their camps 'Hoovervilles', after the President they felt had failed them.

Anacostia Flats

A writer described a visit that he made to the bonus army's camp:

'In the middle of the Anacostia camp is a big platform. Speaking goes on from this platform all morning and all afternoon. The day I saw it a tall scrawny man with deeply sunken cheeks is talking. He's trying to talk about the bonus but he can't stick to it. Before he knows it he's talking about the general economic conditions of the country:
"Here's a plant that can turn out everything every man, woman, and child in this country needs, from potatoes to washing machines, and it's broken down because it can't give the fellow who does the work enough money to buy what he needs with. Give us the money and we'll buy their bread and their corn and beans and their electric iceboxes and their washing machines and their radios. We ain't holding out on 'em because we don't want those things. Can't get a job to make enough money to buy 'em, that's all."'
John Dos Passos, *The Theme is Freedom*, Washington, D.C., 1932.

Dispersing the bonus army

Talk like this alarmed President Hoover. He ordered the army and the police to burn down the bonus marchers' camp and drive them out of Washington. The soldiers carried out Hoover's instructions without much difficulty. But as the smoke billowed up from the burning shacks at Anacostia it seemed to many people that the United States was dangerously close to revolution.

Governor Roosevelt and the Depression

Franklin Roosevelt was sworn-in as Governor of New York State on 1 January 1929, ten months before the Wall Street Crash signalled the start of the Depression.

New York State

The state of which he was now the official head is three times the size of England, and in the early 1930s one out of every ten of the citizens of the United States lived within its borders. It contains one of the world's greatest cities – New York – and other important industrial centres like Buffalo. Such cities have helped to make it one of the United States' leading manufacturing states, with a vast range of products including clothing, textiles, electrical equipment and chemicals.

Roosevelt's policies

As Governor of New York Roosevelt hoped to continue the sort of re-forming social policies pioneered by Al Smith – reducing working hours, for instance, and providing increased compensation for injuries at work. He wished also to provide more help for the aged, the sick and the farmers.

In all these aims Roosevelt achieved something. But the coming of the Depression forced him to postpone many reforms in order to help the unemployed.

Opposition to Roosevelt

Even before this, however, Roosevelt was having trouble with his pol-icies. To turn his aims into achievements he had to persuade the State Legislature to pass laws embodying them – and the State Legislature was controlled by his political opponents, the Republicans.

The New York Republicans distrusted Roosevelt. They particularly disliked his idea that the State government should play a more active part in taking care of its citizens. Like their national leader, President Hoover, they believed that government action of any kind, whether by individual State governments or by the Federal government, should be kept to a minimum. This was the only way, they claimed, to avoid weakening people's ability to stand on their own feet.

Roosevelt and the Depression

This point of view was shared by many New Yorkers in the early stages of Roosevelt's Governorship. But with the lines of unemployed length-ening all over the state, an increasing number came to support Roosevelt's belief that people in difficulties not of their own making had the right to expect the government to help them. Roosevelt put it in these words:

> 'Modern society, acting through its government, owes a definite ob-ligation to prevent the starvation or the dire want of any of its fellow men and women who try to maintain themselves but cannot.
>
> It is true that we have hitherto principally considered those who, through accident or old age, were permanently incapacitated. But the same responsibility of the state undoubtedly applies when wide-spread economic conditions render large numbers of men and women incapable of supporting either themselves or their families because of circumstances beyond their control.'
>
> Governor Franklin D. Roosevelt, 1930.

At the time this statement sounded revolutionary to many people. Yet what alternative was there? The Depression was daily biting deeper into the economic life of New York. With the voluntary systems of un-employment relief beginning to show signs of collapsing under the increasing strain it was clear that only the State government had the power to act on the scale that was needed.

Tackling the Depression

Roosevelt set up a special committee to investigate the problem. He consulted experts of all kinds – factory owners, trade union leaders, economists, social workers – anyone who might have useful information or advice to offer. Then he persuaded the State Legislature to pass a law authorising him to spend twenty million dollars to help the unemployed. New York was the first state in the country to spend public money in this way.

The popularity of Roosevelt's policies with the voters of New York State was shown when he ran for re-election as Governor in 1930. In 1928 he had been elected by a majority of only 25,564 votes; in 1930 he was re-elected with a record majority of 725,001 votes. Laughingly, he remarked to friends that the odd vote in his majority was his own!

Campaigning for President, 1932 : the Democrats decide

The size of Roosevelt's majority in the New York election of 1930, and his active approach to the economic crisis there, made him a strong candidate for nomination as the Democratic party's candidate for President in the Presidential election that was due in 1932.

The 'forgotten man'

A strong candidate, but not the only one. Even within his own party some people distrusted his willingness to abandon old ideas of what government should do and to try new ones. They were disturbed by speeches like one that he had made over the radio in April 1932, in which he said:

> 'These unhappy times call for the building of plans that rest upon the forgotten . . . but . . . indispensable units of economic power, for plans . . . that build from the bottom up and not from the top down, that put their faith once more in the forgotten man at the bottom of the economic pyramid.'
> Governor Franklin D. Roosevelt, April, 1932.

Distrust of Roosevelt

Such speeches as this caused Roosevelt to be accused of trying to stir up the poor – the 'forgotten men' – against the rich. He began to be regarded with suspicion by the more cautious leaders of the Democratic party. Even old political allies like Al Smith began to distrust him, believing that he was too ready to make reckless experiments.

Many others, although they did not particularly distrust Roosevelt, thought that he had neither the ability nor the experience to make a good President. One such observer, the political journalist Walter Lippman, summed him up as 'a pleasant man who, without any important qualification for the office, would very much like to be President'.

The Democratic Convention, 1932

The climax to the campaign to decide who the Democratic presidential candidate should be came in June, 1932. In that month the party's National Convention was held in Chicago.

Roosevelt's opponents made desperate attempts to persuade the Convention to choose some other candidate. Three times a vote was taken, and each time they succeeded in preventing Roosevelt from gaining the two-thirds majority which he needed to become the party's presidential candidate.

Roosevelt's advisers became worried. Unless they could persuade more of the delegates to vote for their man it looked as if someone else would gain the nomination.

Hurriedly arranged meetings were held with the leaders of delegations which had not so far voted for Roosevelt; telephone calls were made; promises were held out; deals were made – and at last the deadlock was broken. The delegates from the large and influential states of California and Texas agreed to give Roosevelt their votes. Another count was made – and he was in!

Campaigning for President, 1932: the nation decides

It was 3 June 1932. A flimsy three-engined aircraft carrying Franklin Roosevelt roared westwards from Albany against strong headwinds.

Accepting the nomination

Several hours later the aircraft bumped down on to the airfield in Chicago and the Roosevelt party drove through cheering crowds to the hall where the Democratic Convention was meeting. Inside the hall Roosevelt braced himself against the speaker's rostrum and stood with his head held high, looking out over the sea of wildly bobbing placards and waving cheerfully in response to the cheers and applause which had greeted his appearance.

A 'new deal'

When the noise died down, Roosevelt began to speak. He accepted the nomination to run for President, and then lashed the country's leaders for their failure to take effective action against the Depression. The Democrats must offer something better, he said; they must become the party 'of the greatest good to the greatest number of our citizens'. Then, in a phrase that would become famous, he told the delegates 'I pledge you, I pledge myself, to a new deal for the American people.'

Roosevelt's chances

After the Convention the delegates scattered to their homes throughout the country. Most were convinced that in Roosevelt they had a certain winner. It was clear by now that many Americans were so angered by the Republican government's failure to halt the Depression that they would vote for the Democratic candidate in the coming election no matter who he was. Roosevelt's advisers were so confident that they believed that all he had to do was to sit back and wait for the Presidency to fall into his lap.

Roosevelt's campaign, 1932

Roosevelt thought differently. He believed that it was important to let people see him in order to disprove rumours that he was not physically fit enough to be President. And, anyway, he loved political campaigning; he certainly did not intend to miss all the excitement and suspense of this campaign, the biggest there was!

'I pledge you, I pledge myself, to a new deal for the American people.' Roosevelt accepts the nomination as the Democratic Party's Presidential candidate at the Chicago Convention in 1932.

Soon after the Chicago Convention a special train carrying Roosevelt and a team of advisers pulled out of Albany and started on a journey from state to state across the continent.

Every day the train made stops where people were waiting to hear Roosevelt. Just before reaching such places he would have his braces fixed on to his legs and, as the train slowed to a halt with its whistle shrieking, he would pull himself stiffly along to the open observation platform at the end of the train. There he would brace himself firmly against the iron guard rail and speak for a few moments to the people who had gathered to meet him. Then, with a cheery wave, he would turn and disappear into the train and off it would go again.

This 'whistle stop' tour across the continent and back again was followed by two more. One took Roosevelt through New England and the other through the southern states. Altogether he travelled over twenty thousand miles, meeting thousands of people and making hundreds of speeches.

The 'brain trust'

Each main speech dealt with some special problem such as unemployment, farming, or taxation. To help to find the right solutions Roosevelt gathered round him a group of experts who came to be known as his 'brain trust'. Many members of the brain trust were university teachers. Their job was to keep Roosevelt informed about the problems they knew most about and to suggest ways in which they might be tackled.

The most important speech of Roosevelt's 1932 campaign was made in the Californian city of San Francisco. There he gave an audience of leading businessmen his ideas about what the government of a modern democratic country should try to do for its citizens.

Roosevelt's social policies

Roosevelt made it quite clear that he believed that the government should not be content to sit on the sidelines of the nation's life as it had done in the 1920s. Instead it should use its power to help its citizens to make better lives for themselves. It should ensure that they were given the chance to earn a fair share of the nation's wealth. It ought to protect their savings so that they could face with confidence the problems of those times of life – 'childhood, sickness, old age' – when money could not be earned. Most important of all, having decided upon the policies the country needed, the government must know how to persuade people to accept them. In a democratic country, Roosevelt claimed, this process of persuading and educating people to support government policies was the statesman's greatest duty.

Reactions to Roosevelt

When it came to the details of how he would achieve his objectives, Roosevelt was usually rather vague. But everywhere he went he left behind an impression of energy and determination, and of caring deeply for the welfare of ordinary people. All over the United States anxious men and women came to feel that here at last was a man who understood their troubles, who sympathised with them – and, most important of all, who sounded as if he would help them. When Roosevelt said 'The country needs and . . demands bold, persistent experimentation . . . above all try something', millions of 'forgotten men' – and women – felt hope stir within them once more after years of despair.

Hoover and Roosevelt

Roosevelt's chief opponent was Herbert Hoover, who was asking American voters to elect him for a second term of office. Where Roosevelt offered hope, Hoover seemed to offer nothing but gloom. 'If you put a rose in Hoover's hand it would wilt,' one observer commented. Hoover condemned the policies of greater government action which Roosevelt was putting forward for he believed that they would only make things worse. They would, he said, 'destroy the very foundations of our American system'. If they were introduced, he prophesied grimly, 'grass will grow in the streets of a hundred cities, a thousand towns'.

Roosevelt wins The majority of the American people ignored Hoover's gloomy warnings. On 9 November 1932, they went to the polling stations and elected Franklin Roosevelt as the next President of the United States by the largest majority in American history. In only six of the nation's forty-eight states did Hoover gain a majority of the votes. In the other forty-two states the people chose Roosevelt.

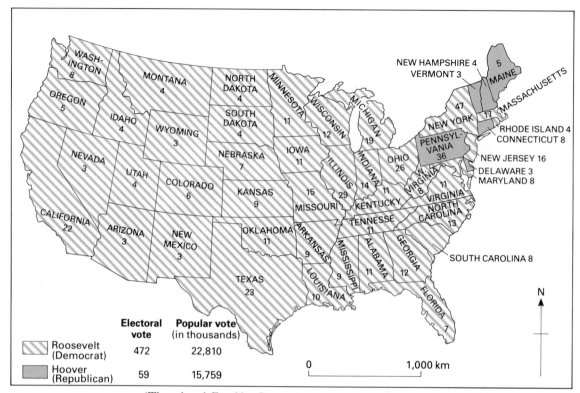

	Electoral vote	Popular vote (in thousands)
Roosevelt (Democrat)	472	22,810
Hoover (Republican)	59	15,759

'They elected Franklin Roosevelt as the next President of the United States by the largest majority in American history.' The result of the 1921 Presidential election. The numbers on the map show the electoral votes of each state in 1932.

9

The First New Deal

Inauguration and the Hundred Days

Inauguration, March 1933

It was 4 March 1933, a cold, grey Saturday with a threat of rain in the air. In front of the white-domed Capitol building in Washington a curious crowd awaited the arrival of Franklin Roosevelt to take the oath of office as President of the United States.

In the four months since Roosevelt's election, the condition of the country had steadily worsened. Hundreds of thousands of Americans were without homes and without sufficient food. Every day saw more of them unemployed – some experts estimated the number now as seventeen million. To many people on that damp Saturday morning it seemed that the whole American way of life was crumbling.

At last Roosevelt appeared. Leaning on the arm of his son Jimmy, he walked stiffly down a red-carpeted ramp to the crowded platform on the steps in front of the Capitol. Here, resting his hand on his own family Bible, he repeated the solemn words of the oath of office.

Then he turned to the crowd. Silently the people before the Capitol and the millions more listening beside their radios waited to hear what he had to offer them.

Roosevelt promises action

Almost immediately Roosevelt struck a note of hope. 'Let me assert my firm belief,' he said, 'that the only thing we have to fear is fear itself.' He promised that the government would give help to the millions of unemployed, to the farmers unable to sell their crops, to those who had lost their homes. 'This nation asks for action, and action now,' he ended.

It was a declaration of war against poverty, hunger and despair. Driving back to the White House, Roosevelt plunged into action. First he called Congress together for a special meeting. Then he acted to end the panic which was paralysing the nation's banking system.

The banking crisis

In the weeks before Roosevelt's inauguration banks all over the country had been forced to close down. With crowds of panic-stricken depositors clamouring to draw out their savings, the banks had found that

'Finis.' As President Hoover walks away from the White House, President Roosevelt throws out the previous government's policies and prepares to make a fresh start. A newspaper cartoon, 3 March 1933.

they did not have enough cash to go round.

Roosevelt ordered all the nation's banks to remain closed while government experts had looked into their affairs. He intended that those which were found to be honestly run and financially sound should be allowed to re-open. If necessary the government would lend them money to see them through their difficulties.

A few days later Congress met and immediately agreed to a plan for reorganising the nation's banking system worked out by Roosevelt's advisers. After this the President spoke over the radio to the American people.

Roosevelt and radio

Today we are used to broadcasts on both radio and television by political leaders, but in the early 1930s such a use of radio was new. Franklin Roosevelt was one of the first to use it effectively to explain his ideas and gain support.

Roosevelt's skill as a radio speaker was one of the secrets of his success, first as Governor and later as President. Here is how one of his advisers described him in action before the microphone:

'His voice and his facial expression as he spoke were those of an intimate friend. After he became President, I often was at the White House when he broadcast, and I realized how unconscious he was of the twenty or thirty of us in the room and how clearly his mind was focused on the people listening at the other end. As he talked his head would nod and his hands would move in simple, natural, comfortable gestures. His face would smile and light up as though he were actually sitting on the front porch or in the parlour with them. People felt this, and it bound them to him in affection.'

Frances Perkins, *The Roosevelt I Knew*, 1946.

The first 'fireside chat'

Roosevelt's broadcast about the banking crisis was more like a talk between friends than a political speech – 'a fireside chat', people called it. 'I want to talk for a few minutes to the American people about banking,' he began, and then explained clearly and simply what had been done to ensure that people could now have confidence in the banks. 'I can assure you,' he told them, 'that it is safer to keep your money in a re-opened bank than under the mattress.'

His listeners believed him. The next day the first banks re-opened and immediately it was clear that the banking crisis was over. The queues of people waiting anxiously to draw out their money disappeared. In some places people even came to put back into the banks the savings they had recently taken out. Roosevelt's first shots in the war against the Depression had hit their mark.

Americans regain confidence

The ending of the banking crisis brought back the nation's confidence. The political journalist who had said that Roosevelt had no qualifications to be president (see page 54) wrote:

'At the beginning of March the country was in such a state of confused despair that it would have followed almost any leader anywhere he chose to go. It was a moment when a dull politician would not have known what to do. By the greatest good fortune which has befallen this country in many a day a kindly and intelligent man had the wit to realize that a great crisis is a great opportunity. He has taken advantage of it. By a series of simple, crisp and orderly measures, he has convinced the country that it need not wait dumbly and miserably for 'the turn', but that it can deal positively and promptly with the difficulties before it. In one week, the nation, which had lost confidence in everything and everybody, has regained confidence in the Government and in itself.'

Walter Lippman, 1933. Reprinted in *Interpretations 1933–1935*, 1936.

The Hundred Days

Roosevelt had no intention of losing this confidence. He sent a stream of proposals for new laws to Congress and most became the law of the land with astonishing speed. Washington had never known anything like it. In the capital's vast government offices the lights burned late, night after night, as shirt-sleeved officials worked into the early hours of the morning thrashing out the details of new schemes for tackling the crisis.

Ending Prohibition

There were other measures, too. In particular, steps were taken to end Prohibition. 'I think this would be a good time for a beer,' said Roosevelt on 12 March, and Congress passed a law making the manufacture and sale of beer legal once more.

A MAN TALKING TO HIS FRIENDS

'To millions of people Roosevelt was their friend.' A newspaper cartoon, 1933. But not everyone felt like this about the President.

Alphabet agencies

But the most important laws passed during these first three months of Roosevelt's administration – 'the Hundred Days', as the period came to be known – were those that set up government organisations called 'agencies' to fight the Depression. Because they were usually referred to by their initials, most people called these the 'alphabet agencies'.

Helping the unemployed: CCC, FERA and CWA

'Our greatest task is to put people to work,' Roosevelt said in his inaugural speech in March 1933. He added that instead of patiently waiting for private firms to provide the jobs that were needed, he was ready to begin 'direct recruiting by the Government itself'.

CCC

The President was particularly concerned about the hundreds of thousands of young men who were wandering the country, often stealing rides on freight trains, in search of work. He set up the first of his alphabet agencies to help such youngsters. It was called the Civilian Conservation Corps (CCC). A magazine reported the news like this:

> '*House Passes Bill for Forestry Jobs*
> A new army of American pioneers will go into the woods within a few weeks. Across 150,000,000 acres of forest lands owned by the Nation and the states, an area five times as large as the state of Connecticut, will march an army of workers, now unemployed and trudging city streets.
>   It is estimated that under the plans of the Roosevelt Unemployment Conservation Bill, signed by the President last week, 250,000 men can shortly be put to work on reforestation. That this army will be fully enlisted . . . was evident from the rain of applications that poured into Washington from all over the country.'
>
> *Newsweek* magazine, 8 April 1933.

By August 1933, the CCC had housed 250,000 young men in camps all over the country. They were hard at work cutting fire lanes through forests, strengthening river banks, and planting trees in areas threatened by soil erosion. The government gave the CCC workers food and shelter and paid them a dollar a day. Many sent most of their wages home to help their families. 'It sure beats "Brother, can you spare a dime?",' said one of them.

FERA

Fast action was also needed to feed, to clothe and to snelter the millions of unemployed. To help with these problems Congress passed the Federal Emergency Relief Act (FERA). This gave 500 million dollars to provide food and other necessities for the unemployed. The distribution of the money was left to the governments of the individual states.

Harry Hopkins

The President chose a young social worker named Harry Hopkins to run FERA. Hopkins had been in charge of organising 'relief' – that is, help for the poor – for Roosevelt in New York State. 'I'm here to see that people don't starve,' Hopkins said simply when he arrived in Washington.

In his first two hours as head of FERA Hopkins gave out five million dollars. But he soon began to feel that to regain their confidence and self-respect, the unemployed needed jobs, not hand-outs. So he persuaded the President to put him in charge of another alphabet agency, the Civil Works Administration (CWA).

CWA

By the January of 1934 Hopkins had found work for four million people. But critics claimed that although CWA provided people with a wage to live on, the work it gave them was often of little value. In 1935, therefore, it was replaced by a more carefully thought out organisation, again run by Hopkins, called the Works Progress Administration, or WPA. You can read more about this later (see page 77).

Helping the farmers: AAA

In April 1933, a disturbing story appeared in American newspapers. It told how farmers in the mid-western state of Iowa had seized a judge who was hearing a case against a farmer who couldn't afford to keep up the mortgage payments on his farm. They had dragged the judge from his court house and nearly lynched him.

Farming and the Depression

The incident was just one sign of the growing anger of American farmers. By 1933 their position had become desperate. The income of the average farmer was now less than one-third of what it had been in 1929 – and farmers had been badly off even then. Many were leaving their crops to rot in the fields, because selling prices were too low to cover the costs of harvesting them.

Roosevelt had spoken about this problem a year earlier, in his 'forgotten man' radio speech of April 1932:

'Approximately one-half of our whole population, fifty or sixty million people, earn their living by farming or in small towns whose existence depends on farms. They have today lost their purchasing power. Why? They are receiving for farm products less than the cost to them of growing these farm products. The result of this loss of purchasing power is that many other millions of people engaged in industry in the cities cannot sell industrial products to the farming half of the Nation. This brings home to every city worker [the fact that] his own employment is directly tied up with [the] farmer's dollar. No Nation can long endure half bankrupt. Main Street, Broadway, the mills, the mines will close if half the buyers are broke.

I cannot escape the conclusion that one of the essential parts of a national program of restoration must be to restore purchasing power to the farming half of the country.'

Governor Franklin D. Roosevelt, radio broadcast, April 1932.

AAA

With lawlessness threatening to sweep the countryside, Roosevelt made helping the farmers another of his government's most urgent tasks. Early in May 1933, Congress passed a law setting up a government agency called the Agricultural Adjustment Administration, or the AAA.

The main aim of the AAA was to raise farmers' incomes. To achieve this, government experts decided that the production of meat, corn, cotton and other leading farm goods would have to be limited. If smaller quantities were produced, argued Roosevelt's Secretary of Agriculture, Henry Wallace, prices would be higher and farmers would be better off. Those farmers who agreed to grow less corn or cotton would be given money by the government to make up for having less to sell.

Reducing farm production

So the AAA bought and destroyed five million pigs. In southern states like Mississippi and Texas it paid farmers to plough thousands of hectares of cotton into the ground. These cotton farmers faced a practical problem. The mules that pulled their ploughs had been taught to walk between the rows of cotton plants; now they had to be persuaded to trample right over them.

There was much bitter criticism of the AAA's policies. To many people it seemed stupid and even wicked that, at a time when so many people were hungry, the government should actually be paying farmers not to grow food. Nevertheless, the AAA's policies achieved their aim. Year by year the prices of farm products crept upward.

Wheat, for instance, sold at 33 cents a bushel in 1933; by 1934 it was selling at 69 cents, by 1935 at 89 cents and by 1937 at well over a dollar (that is, 100 cents). As a result of such increases, by 1936 farmers' incomes were half as high again as they had been in 1933.

The second AAA

As you can read later (see page 85), in 1936 the Supreme Court declared that the AAA was unconstitutional. But both the President and Congress believed that its central idea of controlling crop surpluses was vital to the prosperity of the nation's farmers. In 1938, therefore, Congress passed a second Agricultural Adjustment Act to take its place.

Helping industry: PWA and NRA

When Roosevelt became President in 1933, American factories were producing in value less than half of what they had produced in 1929. As sales of manufactured goods fell employers everywhere were cutting wages and dismissing workers in a desperate attempt to save their businesses from collapse. Such actions only made the situation worse. As both wages and the number of people employed were reduced, so was the nation's purchasing power. The result was that even fewer goods were bought, and industry's position became still more desperate.

PWA

By June 1933, Roosevelt's advisers had worked out a plan to meet this crisis. It was passed by Congress with the title of the National Industrial Recovery Act. One part of the new act set up another alphabet agency called the Public Works Administration, or PWA.

The PWA was headed by an energetic and sharp-tongued lawyer named Harold Ickes. Its aim was to create work for some of the millions of industrial workers who were unable to get jobs.

The PWA concentrated on heavy construction work such as building roads, dams and bridges. One of its proudest achievements was the completion of a huge dam on the Colorado River in the west of the United States. Work on this had begun when Hoover was President. It had originally been intended to name it after him, but Ickes rather unkindly decided to call it Boulder Dam instead. In later years, however, it was renamed the Hoover Dam.

One of the main aims of the PWA was to create purchasing power and so help private industry to recover from the Depression by providing people with the money to buy its products. But increasing consumer purchasing power was not the only aim of the National Industrial Recovery Act. Another part of the act set up a government agency called the National Recovery Administration, or NRA.

NRA

The NRA set out to persuade employers in particular industries to get together and draw up sets of rules called 'codes'. All the firms in each industry were then asked to obey the rules laid down in their code about such things as minimum wages and maximum hours for workers. Those firms which agreed to do this were given permission to advertise the fact by displaying the special badge of the NRA – a picture of a blue eagle with outspread wings, bearing beneath it the motto 'We do our part'.

The aim of the NRA codes was to end the cut-throat competition which had been sending both wages and prices spiralling downwards. This is how Roosevelt explained the idea in one of his fireside chats:

'If all employers in each competitive group agree to pay their workers the same wages – reasonable wages – and require the same hours – reasonable hours – then higher wages and shorter hours will hurt no employer. Moreover, such action is better for the employer than unemployment and low wages, because it makes more buyers for his product. That is the simple idea which is at the very heart of the Industrial Recovery Act [NRA].'

President Franklin D. Roosevelt, radio broadcast, June 1933.

Support for NRA

At first Americans were wildly enthusiastic about the NRA. In San Francisco eight thousand children lined up on a baseball ground to form an NRA eagle and newspapers reported that girls were even having eagles tatooed on their backs!

Weaknesses of NRA

But soon the NRA was in trouble. One weakness of its codes was that no employer could be compelled by law to obey the rules they laid down. Some employers – Henry Ford was one – simply ignored them. Others pretended to accept the codes, but failed to keep their rules.

"DON'T TELL ME IT ISN'T WORKING."

NRA

SECRETARY PERKINS
REPORTS
$40,000,000
GAINS IN WEEKLY
PAYROLLS

2,2000,000
PUT BACK TO WORK
IN LAST 5 MONTHS.

750,000
RETURN TO
JOBS DURING
AUGUST.

A pro-Roosevelt newspaper cartoonist looks at the work of the NRA, 18 September 1933.

Some refused to pay the minimum wages that had been agreed upon. Others tried to use the codes as a way of raising prices.

Tricks such as these caused many workers to lose their enthusiasm for the NRA. Employers, too, had complaints. They particularly disliked the fact that the National Industrial Recovery Act gave workers the legal right to form trade unions – labor unions, as Americans called them. Many workers were eager to take advantage of this right. But some employers refused to recognise the unions and a wave of strikes swept industrial areas. In many places fighting broke out between workers struggling to obtain their rights and guards hired by their employers.

Other Hundred Days reforms

One day early in the New Deal, this letter arrived at the White House in Washington:

'Dear Mr. President,

This is just to tell you everything is all right now. The man you sent found our house all right and we went down to the bank with him and the mortgage can go on for a while longer. You remember I wrote you about losing the furniture too. Well, your man got it back for us. I never heard of a President like you, Mr Roosevelt. Mrs. --- and I are old folks and don't amount to much, but we are joined with those millions of others in praying for you every night. God bless you, Mr. Roosevelt.'

Quoted in John Gunther, *Roosevelt in Retrospect*, 1950.

HOLC

The rescue act that this writer is describing was made possible by another Hundred Days law. This set up an agency called the Home Owners' Loan Corporation (HOLC), which provided long term loans for people who were finding it difficult to meet mortgage payments on their homes. During the middle 1930s the HOLC helped almost 1,000 families a day to keep a roof over their heads.

FCA

Another Hundred Days law set up the Farm Credit Administration (FCA). This provided farmers with low interest loans, so that they could pay off their debts and keep their farms. In the middle 1930s the FCA helped as many as 300 farmers a day to hold on to their land.

Shares and banks

The Federal Securities Act tightened the rules about selling shares, to stop the sort of dishonesty that had helped to cause the Wall Street Crash of 1929. A banking act set up the Federal Deposit Insurance Corporation (FDIC), which to this day insures Americans' savings against the possible collapse of the banks in which they are deposited.

But the boldest experiment of all to be authorised during the Hundred Days was none of these. That distinction belongs to the Tennessee Valley Authority, TVA, whose story is told in the next chapter.

10

Restoring a Region: TVA

The Tennessee Valley problem

The Tennessee river in the eastern United States drains an area as large as that of England and Scotland. In 1933, fed by one of the heaviest rainfalls in north America, it often caused widespread flooding. Its valley had once been covered by trees, but generations of farmers cut down the trees and ploughed the valley slopes. The farmers' crops of maize, tobacco and cotton exhausted the land, taking nourishment from it but giving nothing back. All were crops planted in the spring and harvested in the autumn, so that in winter the fields lay bare. In many places the land became eroded and useless when its soil was washed away by the heavy winter rains.

A British scientist who visited the area in the early 1930s described what he saw:

'The erosion was appalling. It was brought home to me when I was told that there were men still living who remembered the Tennessee River as a clear blue stream. Up till that moment I had taken the pea-soup appearance of so many American rivers for a fact of nature; the realisation that it was man-made was staggering.

Here, under my eyes, was the basic productivity being stripped from a vast area and hurried along to waste in the sea. I saw out-crops of bare rock which three generations back had been covered with rich soil over a yard in depth. The amount of soil annually washed or blown out of the fields of the United States is estimated at 3,000 million tons.'

Julian Huxley, *TVA: Adventure in Planning*, 1943.

Shortly after his election as President, Roosevelt made a tour of the Tennessee Valley in the company of Senator George Norris. Norris had for thirty years been pressing without success for the Federal government to sponsor a scheme to deal with the valley's problems. The tour reinforced Roosevelt's determination to make helping the Tennessee Valley one of the first tasks of his new government.

'The most urgent task was to halt soil erosion.' Badly eroded land in the Tennessee Valley in the early 1930s.

TVA's plans and dams

TVA's aims

During the Hundred Days, President Roosevelt persuaded Congress to set up the Tennessee Valley Authority. TVA's first aim was to bring the waters of the Tennessee under control, to lessen the danger of flooding and make the river more useful for shipping. Its second aim was to use the power of the river to make electricity. Its third was to plant trees and introduce new ways of farming in order to make the land productive again.

Flood control and electricity

The Tennessee was tamed by building a chain of dams along the river and its tributaries to control the flow of their waters. As well as preventing flooding the dams also produced hydro-electricity as the waters of their man-made lakes rushed through spinning turbines. Before this only two out of every hundred farms in the TVA region had electric light and power. But TVA sold its electricity very cheaply and this helped the farmers of the Tennessee Valley to modernise their methods and increase the comfort of their homes.

TVA's electricity helped, too, in the growth of industry. Factories were set up to make chemicals, including cheap fertilisers. Other factories produced paper, aluminium and flour. Such industries brought new jobs and prosperity to the people of the Tennessee Valley.

Saving the land

Any farmer depends for success on his soil. With good soil he can prosper, producing plentiful crops and healthy livestock. With poor soil he can do little but struggle to make ends meet. So the TVA's farming experts turned first to the soil in their attempts to help the Tennessee Valley's farmers.

Halting erosion

The most urgent task was to halt erosion, the washing away of the farmer's soil by rain. The best way to do this was to give the land a cover of plant life, whose roots would hold the soil in place in times of heavy rain.

One way of giving cover to the earth is to plant trees and this was done on a vast scale all over the Tennessee Valley. Another way was to persuade farmers to plant more crops such as grass and clover, which would keep the ground covered all the year round. If farmers wished to go on growing arable crops, they had to be persuaded to plough their furrows across hillsides instead of up and down them. This is called contour ploughing and makes sure that rain is held in the ground instead of running away down the furrows, washing the soil along with it.

Fertilisers

But halting erosion was not the only thing needed to make the valley's farms prosperous. In many places the soil needed feeding, for years of over-cropping had left it exhausted. Here again TVA helped. It sold the farmers cheap fertilisers made in factories powered by its electricity.

Persuading the farmers

The TVA's experts had answers to the farmers' problems; their next task was to persuade the farmers to adopt them, for TVA had no power to force anyone to accept its advice.

From 1933 'test demonstration farms' were set up in different parts of the valley. These were farms whose owners agreed to accept the advice and help of the TVA's experts.

The neighbours of demonstration farmers soon saw the difference which the new methods made. They saw crop yields increasing. They watched cattle grazing on green fields that had once been eroded and barren. More and more became demonstration farmers and the fields and hills of the Tennessee Valley became green again as the washing away of the top soil was halted. Soon it became one of the proudest boasts of the TVA that the water now ran blue again between its dams.

Democracy at work

Criticism of TVA

In the 1930s TVA had many critics as well as many admirers. Privately owned power companies in the area objected to the Federal government using tax payers' money to produce cheap electricity; they argued that such competition was unfair to them. Other critics went further. They claimed that TVA was a trial run for a communist scheme to undermine the American capitalist way of life by replacing private ownership of the nation's resources by state control.

TVA's significance

Despite such criticisms TVA went on with its work and it is still operating today. It has helped to make life better for millions of people.

But this is not the only reason why one admirer described TVA as 'the greatest single American invention of this century'. Just as important as its achievements is the democratic way in which they have been won.

TVA showed how a nation could bring about great economic and social changes by persuasion rather than by force. In the 1930s, when the people of some countries were abandoning democratic forms of

'Democracy at the grass roots.' A farmer gives his vote for or against a new TVA cotton-marketing plan.

government and accepting the rule of dictators in a desperate attempt to escape from poverty and unemployment, it was a practical demonstration of what a democratic way of doing things could achieve.

Grass roots democracy

Instead of giving people less say in running their lives, as happened in dictatorships, the TVA gave them more. It encouraged them to set up their own co-operative groups – to sell the electricity produced by TVA, for instance, or to organise the marketing of farm produce. These co-operatives were run by the people of the valley themselves and gave them valuable experience of what was called 'democracy at the grass roots' – democracy at work in everyday life.

Roosevelt himself regarded this aspect of TVA as one of its most important features. In September 1940, at a time when the all-conquering armies of the German dictator Hitler seemed about to destroy the last remains of democracy in Europe, Roosevelt travelled to the Tennessee Valley to open a new dam. In a speech he explained how TVA was an example of democracy at work:

'These fine changes we see have not come by compulsion – for . . . thousands of townspeople have met together in the common effort. They have debated it and discussed it. Participating in the processes of their government – State government, local government, Federal government – they have altered the looks of their towns and their counties. They have added fertilizer to the soil. They have improved their industries.

No farmer was forced to join this conservation movement. No workman was compelled to labour here . . . for less than a rightful wage. No citizen has lost a single one of these human liberties that we prize so highly. This is a demonstration of what a democracy at work can do . . .'

President Franklin D. Roosevelt, September 1940.

11

The Second New Deal

Opponents of the New Deal

'He was God in this country.' Those words, spoken by a New York taxi driver during a 1960s television interview, summed up the way that millions of poorer Americans had come to feel about Franklin Roosevelt by the middle of the 1930s.

The rich and Roosevelt

But millions of other Americans had very different feelings about the President. Many saw him as a threat to their whole way of life and feared and hated everything that he stood for. This was especially true of the rich, partly because Roosevelt had made them pay higher taxes in order to help to pay for his reforms. In April, 1936, *Time* magazine wrote:

> 'Regardless of party and regardless of region, today, with few exceptions, members of the so-called Upper Class frankly hate Franklin Roosevelt.'
>
> *Time* magazine, April 1936.

Criticisms of Roosevelt

But many opposed the President for less selfish reasons. Some were alarmed at the vast sums of money which his government was spending on such things as public works. The country could not afford such spending, they cried, and claimed that much of the money was being wasted anyway. Some said that the spending was a form of bribery, and that Roosevelt was using it to buy people's support. Others feared that his policies would destroy people's ability to stand on their own feet. It was wrong, they claimed, to give people government help against poverty and unemployment; they ought to provide for such needs themselves.

Federal power

But perhaps the most powerful reason for opposition to the President was fear of the growing power of the Federal government. Many Americans believed that under Roosevelt it was interfering too much in people's lives. Moreover, Roosevelt's policies seemed to be threatening

An anti-Roosevelt cartoon, April, 1938. In what way is it criticising the New Deal?

the tradition that the Federal authorities should leave as much of the work of government as possible to the individual states.

At the head of this ever-more powerful Federal government one man stood alone – Franklin Delano Roosevelt. 'We have to turn back many centuries,' claimed one of his opponents, 'to find so great a power over the lives of millions of men lodged in the hands of a single fallible being.'

Father Coughlin

However, some of Roosevelt's critics attacked him not for doing too much, but for doing too little. Father Charles Coughlin was a Catholic priest with a radio programme that attracted ten million listeners a week in the early 1930s. Before the 1932 election Coughlin had supported Roosevelt, telling his listeners that the choice that faced them was 'Roosevelt or ruin'. But soon he was calling the President 'Franklin Double-Crossing Roosevelt' and attacking him for not providing enough help for the poor.

The Townsend Plan

Francis E. Townsend, a retired doctor in California, also criticised Roosevelt for doing too little. He was particularly concerned about the problems that the Depression was causing for old people and in 1934 called upon the government to pay everyone over the age of sixty a pension of 200 dollars a month. In return pensioners would have to do two things. The first was to retire immediately and so free millions of jobs for other people. The second was to spend the whole of their pension within a month and so make the country's shops and factories busy again. In this way, Townsend claimed, his plan would end the Depression.

Huey Long

But Roosevelt's most dangerous political rival in the middle 1930s was Senator Huey Long, the former Governor of the state of Louisiana. The Kingfish, as Long called himself, had ruled Louisiana almost as a dictator. But he had shown genuine concern for the state's many poor and had taxed oil companies and other wealthy businesses to pay for changes which benefited them. He had built bridges across rivers, roads through swamps, set up night schools which taught 175,000 illiterate adults to read. 'I'm a small fish here in Washington,' Long told reporters when he arrived to take up his position as Senator. 'But I'm the Kingfish to the folks down in Louisiana.'

'Share Our Wealth'

Long claimed that Roosevelt's New Deal had failed to share out the nation's wealth fairly. In 1935 he announced his own plans to do this under the slogan 'Share Our Wealth'.

A 1930s WPA team build a road which will link a lonely farm with a market town.

Long said that the government should confiscate the 'swollen fortunes' of the rich and use the money to give every American family a house, a car and an income of between two and three thousand dollars a year. This is how he explained his ideas in a 1935 radio broadcast:

'All the people of America have been invited to a barbecue. God invited us all to come and eat and drink all we wanted. He smiled on our land and we grew crops of plenty to eat and wear.

He showed us the earth, the iron and other things to make anything we wanted. He unfolded to us the secrets of science so that our work might be easy. God called: "Come to my feast."

Then what happened? Rockefeller, Morgan [millionaire businessmen] and their crowd stepped up and took enough for 120,000,000 people and left only enough for 5,000,000, for all the 125,000,000 to eat. And so many millions must go hungry and without these good things God gave us – unless we call on them to put some of it back.'

Huey Long broadcast, reported in the
New York Times, 10 January 1935.

Long's promise to make 'every man a king' attracted the support of millions, especially among the very poor. He began planning to challenge Roosevelt for the Presidency in the 1936 election. Before he could do so, however, he was shot and killed by a young man who was said to have a personal grudge against him. And without the Kingfish, the 'Share Our Wealth' movement gradually faded away.

More help for the unemployed: WPA

Despite the reforms of the first three years of the New Deal, millions of Americans were still unemployed in 1935. Roosevelt decided that only a still bigger programme of public works could bring about further economic recovery. He therefore persuaded Congress to set up another alphabet agency to organise such a programme and gave Harry Hopkins the job of running it. The new agency was called the Works Progress Administration, or WPA.

WPA in action

The aim of the WPA was to set people to work on jobs which would be valuable to the community. By 1937 its chiefs were able to point proudly to the 11,000 schools and other public buildings which their workers had erected; to the 43,000 miles of road they had built; and to many other useful achievements. Unemployed writers produced guide books to the country's states and cities; artists painted murals on the walls of post offices and town halls; groups of actors toured the country to perform their plays; and thousands of students were found part-time jobs so that they could afford to continue their studies.

The WPA did not end unemployment in the United States. But altogether, between 1935 and 1941, it gave useful work to an average of two million Americans a year. It was not only the wages these people earned that were important to them. Once they had a job and experienced again the satisfaction of doing something useful, they regained their self-respect.

'Priming the pump'

The money earned by WPA and other alphabet agency workers began to bring trade and business back to life. Shops had more customers. Sales of food and clothing, especially, began to rise. As people started to buy again, shopkeepers, farmers and manufacturers began to benefit from the money the government was spending. This process was described by Roosevelt as 'priming the pump'. By this he meant that the government money was acting like a fuel, flowing into the nation's economic machinery and starting it moving again.

But to work really well the nation's economic machinery needed more than refuelling. Some of its parts were worn out and obsolete. Roosevelt believed that the only way to ensure that it would never again break down so disastrously was to complete the work of modernising it begun by Theodore Roosevelt and Woodrow Wilson. This work of modernisation was the New Deal's next task.

Improvements for workers

Under the American system of government, the Supreme Court – the highest law court in the land – has the power to decide whether laws passed by Congress are legal or not. In 1935 the Court declared that the National Industrial Recovery Act of 1933 was illegal. By this time it had become clear that, as far as the NRA codes were concerned, the 1933 act was a flop (see page 66). But this was not true of other parts of the act and the government immediately introduced new laws so that these would be able to continue.

The Wagner Act, 1935

One of the most important of these new 1935 laws was the Wagner Act. This was named after Senator Robert Wagner of New York, the man who first persuaded Roosevelt that it was needed and then guided it through the Senate. The Wagner Act restated the right of workers to join labor unions and forbade employers to penalise those who did so. It also set up a new government body called the National Labor Relations Board to try to see that the new law was obeyed.

John L. Lewis

The Board's task was not an easy one. Many employers were still determined not to recognise labor unions. But, with the Federal government's support, workers all over the United States successfully demanded their rights. In 1936 their position was further strengthened when a fiery-tempered miners' leader named John L. Lewis welded together a number of separate unions into a giant new organisation, later named the Congress of Industrial Organizations.

The CIO

The CIO was based on an idea called 'industrial unionism' – that is, that all workers in a particular industry should belong to the same union, whatever their particular skill or trade. To the tune of a famous patriotic song called 'The Battle Hymn of the Republic', CIO members sang these words:

> 'It is we who plowed the prairies, built the cities where they trade,
> Dug the mines and built the workshops, endless miles of railroad laid;
> Now we stand outcast and starving mid the wonders we have made
> But the union makes us strong!
>
> Solidarity forever!
> Solidarity forever!
> Solidarity forever!
> For the union makes us strong!'

CIO union song, 1937.

More union members

In the later 1930s labor union membership increased rapidly, as workers came to realise that with a powerful union they had a much better chance of obtaining higher wages and improved working conditions. In 1933 American labor unions had only three million members. By the end of 1937 they had over seven million and by 1939 over nine million. Many of these extra millions were members of unions in the new CIO group, while others belonged to an older group of unions called the American Federation of Labor.

The Fair Labor Standards Act, 1938

In 1938 the government again showed its sympathetic attitude towards the needs of the workers. Roosevelt's supporters forced the Fair Labor Standards Act through Congress. This laid down maximum hours of work and minimum wages in many industries. It also forbade the employment of children under the age of sixteen in most jobs, except farming.

The Fair Labor Standards Act resulted in pay increases for some three hundred thousand employees and in a shorter working week for well over a million more. In later years, when the act was extended to include additional jobs of various kinds, still more people benefited.

Providing security: the Social Security Act

Frances Perkins

The Secretary of Labor in Roosevelt's New Deal administration was Frances Perkins, the first woman ever to hold such a high position in an American government. For her, providing people with security against poverty was a top priority. It was so important to her that she only accepted Roosevelt's offer of a job in his government when he agreed to her ideas for a national scheme of old age and unemployment insurance.

The Social Security Act, 1935

In September 1935, with help from Senator Wagner, Frances Perkins persuaded Congress to pass the Social Security Act. This was, in fact, several laws in one. First, it gave government support to a plan to provide pensions for old people and for widows. It also made arrangements for the Federal and State governments to join together to help other people who were in need and unable to help themselves, such as the blind, the orphaned and children with handicaps.

Unemployment insurance

But perhaps the most important part of the Social Security Act was that which, for the first time in the United States, set up a national system of unemployment insurance. This was to be run by the individual states and meant that people in a wide range of occupations would receive at least a small income if they lost their jobs. The money to pay for these benefits was to come from special taxes paid by both workers and employers. Although at first not all workers were covered by the new scheme, as the years passed more were able to take advantage of it.

Critics of Social Security

One group of critics of the Social Security Act thought that it did not do enough to help the elderly and the jobless. They argued that too many workers – those working on farms or for firms with fewer than eight employees for example – were not eligible to take part. They also criticised the low payments made under the scheme and the fact that it would take several years to bring fully into operation.

Other people criticised the act because it did too much rather than too little. One critic said that government insurance ideas would ruin the nation 'by destroying initiative, discouraging thrift and stifling individual responsibility'. Another wrote this about the act:

> 'It is begging the unfit to be more unfit. Even such a measure as old-age insurance, which I am sure must touch the sympathies of every one, . . . removes one of the points of pressure which has kept many persons up to the strife and struggle of life.'
>
> American Liberty League pamphlet, January 1936.

Despite such criticisms the Social Security Act proved to be one of the most lasting of Roosevelt's New Deal reforms. With various additions and amendments it continues to be the law of the United States today. According to Frances Perkins, Roosevelt 'took greater satisfaction from it than anything else achieved on the domestic front'.

12

The Later New Deal

The 1936 Presidential election

In the 1936 Presidential election the opportunity came for Roosevelt's critics to put their points of view to the American people. Roosevelt's chief opponent for the Presidency was the Republican party's Alfred Landon, the Governor of the state of Kansas.

Roosevelt's opponents

Landon himself was a moderate Republican who agreed with some parts of the New Deal. But his supporters attacked not only Roosevelt's policies, but the man himself. He was a would-be dictator, warned some, out to turn the American people into the slaves of an all-powerful state. He was ruining the country, claimed others, by his reckless spending. He was a madman, whispered a few, driven onwards by an insane lust for personal power.

Roosevelt's supporters

The attacks were in vain. To millions of voters Roosevelt, no matter what his opponents said, could do no wrong. Many of these people – farmers, for example – had often not supported the Democratic party in the past. But they saw Roosevelt as the man who had given them jobs, who had saved their homes, their farms, their savings. To them the New Deal and the man who had created it were not things to be feared; they were things to be thankful for.

The 1936 campaign

In the 1936 election such people turned Roosevelt's campaign journeys into triumphant processions. When the votes were counted in November it was found that Roosevelt had swept the country. He had won all but two of the nation's forty-eight states and had been re-elected as President by the largest majority of popular votes in American history.

Dust Bowl refugees

As a result of the policies of such organisations as the AAA (see page 65) and TVA (see page 69) the New Deal made many American farmers better off. Generally speaking, those who benefited most were those who owned their land.

Tenants and sharecroppers

But many farmers were tenants or sharecroppers, farming land owned by other people. The early New Deal's crop limitation policies (see page 71) had actually worsened their position. By reducing the amount of cultivated land the AAA sometimes forced them off the land they worked. And while the land's owners were paid by the government for not producing, the displaced tenants and sharecroppers received nothing. Many who managed to hang on to their jobs and their homes lost both when the owners of land still being worked decided to cultivate it with tractors, a more profitable method. As machines replaced people on the land, a black blues singer and sharecropper sang:

'Now you ought to cut off so many trucks and tractors,
White folks, you ought to work more mules and men,
Then you know that would make, ooh babe,
Money get thick again.'
Song 'Working Man Blues' by Sleepy John Estes, 1940.

Dust storms

Nature added to tenant farmers' problems. In parts of the south and the middle west of the United States the soil was exhausted from years of careless farming. In 1933 these areas suffered a prolonged drought. Over thousands of square kilometres the sun turned the soil into light and lifeless dust. Then came strong winds, picking up the dust and swirling it away in choking clouds. A writer who witnessed one of these great dust storms described it like this:

'By mid-morning a gale was blowing, cold and black. By noon it was blacker than night, because one can see through night and this was . . . a wall of dirt one's eyes could not penetrate, but it could penetrate the eyes and ears and nose. It could penetrate to the lungs until one coughed up black . . .

When the wind died and the sun shone forth again, it was on a different world. There were no fields, only sand drifting into mounds. . . . There was no longer a . . . road fifty feet from the front door. It was obliterated. In the farmyard, fences, machinery were gone, buried. The roofs of sheds stuck out through drifts deeper than a man is tall.'
R. S. D. Lusk, *The Saturday Evening Post* magazine,
13 August 1938.

Okie migrants

Faced with conditions like this there was often only one thing for the farmers to do. They packed what they could carry on to their battered old Tin Lizzies and moved out. Because many of these refugees from the tractors and the dust storms came from the state of Oklahoma, people called them 'Okies'. From 1933 onwards thousands of them went westward, hoping that beyond the Rocky Mountains in California they would find some way of making a living.

The Okies were often disappointed. The people of California looked with suspicion and sometimes with fear upon the thousands of ragged strangers pouring down from the mountains into their towns and villages. Often the only work to be found was fruit and vegetable picking. Both jobs were badly paid and short-lasting, and the lives of most of the 'dust bowl' refugees continued to be hard.

Dorothea Lange

In the spring of 1936 it was so cold in California that the crops were freezing in the fields. A photographer named Dorothea Lange remembered meeting a woman there:

> 'I saw and approached the hungry and desperate mother as if drawn by a magnet. I do not remember how I explained my presence or my camera to her, but I do remember she asked me no questions . . . She told me her age, that she was 32. She said that they had been living on frozen vegetables from the surrounding fields, and birds that the children had killed. She had just sold the tires from the car to buy food. There she sat in that lean-to tent with her children huddled around her and seemed to know that my picture might help her and so she helped me. There was a sort of equality about it.'
>
> Dorothea Lange, 'The Assignment I'll Never Forget',
> *Popular Photography*, February 1960.

You can see the photograph that Lange took of the migrant mother and her children on page 84.

More help for farmers: FSA

FSA in action

Dorothea Lange was given a job by a government agency called the Farm Security Administration (FSA). The FSA was set up in 1937 to remedy the shortcomings of the AAA. Its main job was to provide loans to help tenant farmers and sharecroppers to buy farms and equipment. By 1940 it had made short-term loans to more than 800,000 farming families and long-term loans to buy farms to another 13,600.

The FSA employed photographers like Dorothea Lange to make city people – and members of Congress – more aware of the sufferings of the rural poor. It allowed newspapers and magazines to print the photographs without charge. In an age before television these pictures brought home to millions what it was like to be really poor during the Depression.

Only when the outbreak of the Second World War made Californian factories begin to take on more workers, did life start to improve for the dust bowl migrants. Busy wartime factories gave what the land had denied them – well-paid and lasting work.

Improving farm incomes

Yet despite the hard times experienced by many farming families in the 1930s, those who managed to hold on to their land gradually saw things improving. By 1939 incomes from farming had more than dou-

Migrant mother and children photographed in California by Dorothea Lange in 1936.

bled since 1932. Most of this increase was the result of a steady rise in the prices of farm products.

Farmers and the New Deal

Roosevelt's opponents argued that this rise was as much a result of the shortages caused by the dust-storms and the droughts as it was of the government's policies. Most farmers thought differently. They believed that on the whole the AAA, the FSA and the government's other New Deal measures had helped to make life better for them. They were receiving higher prices for their crops. Their futures had been made more secure by government-supported schemes of crop insurance. Their home lives had been made more comfortable and their farming easier by the Rural Electrification Administration, a government scheme for bringing electricity into rural areas. It is not surprising, therefore, that throughout the 1930s farmers, like industrial workers, were amongst Roosevelt's strongest supporters.

The Supreme Court struggle

After his victory in the 1936 election Roosevelt began his second term as President eager to continue the New Deal. Although things had improved since the dark days of 1932, there was still much to do. 'I see one-third of a nation ill-housed, ill-clad, ill-nourished,' he said in his inaugural speech.

The National Housing Act, 1937

In 1937 Congress passed the National Housing Act, under which the Federal government provided money to build new homes for low income families. The act set up the United States' Housing Authority. Within a few years this had built 150,000 new houses and flats for poor families to rent.

The Supreme Court

But blocking further progress along the road of reform stood an obstacle – the Supreme Court of the United States. As you have read already (page 9), all the laws passed by Congress have to meet certain conditions laid down in the Constitution, and the power of deciding whether any particular law meets the Constitution's conditions belongs to the Supreme Court.

Even before the 1936 election the Supreme Court had shown a hostile attitude towards a number of New Deal laws. We have seen how, in 1935, it declared the NIRA to be illegal. In 1936 the same thing happened to the AAA. Now, in 1937, the fate of such other key laws as the Social Security Act was in doubt.

Roosevelt's reform plan

To Roosevelt it seemed wrong that the Justices of the Supreme Court, who were not elected by the people, should be able to stop the introduction of laws which both he and Congress thought the nation needed. At that time there were nine of these Justices and a majority of them usually voted against the New Deal laws. To get round their opposition Roosevelt planned to appoint additional Justices to the Court, who would support the new laws and thus make it possible for him to continue his reforming policies.

Opposition to Roosevelt's plan

When Roosevelt suggested his plan to Congress in February 1937, there was a tremendous outcry against it. It was clear that for once the President had misjudged popular opinion. Even people who usually supported him spoke out against his plan.

The trouble was that it looked too much like a scheme to destroy the Supreme Court's independence, by filling it with Roosevelt's own supporters. Even people who had been irritated by many of the Court's recent decisions did not want this to happen. His opponents had even stronger feelings on the matter. It was by tampering with the law courts and the rules of government that the dictator Hitler had recently succeeded in destroying democracy in Germany. Roosevelt's old rival, Herbert Hoover, spoke for many Americans when he said that he did not want to open the way for the same kind of thing to happen in the United States:

'. . . Liberty is crumbling over two-thirds of the world. In less than a score of years the courts in a dozen nations have been made subject to political power, and . . . the people's securities in those countries have gone out of the window. And, mark you this – in every instance the persuaders have professed to be acting for the people and in the name of progress. As we watch the parade of nations down that suicide road every American has cause to be anxious for our republic.

. . . We have already gone far on the road of personal government. The American people must halt when it is proposed to lay hands on the independence of the Supreme Court. It is the last safeguard of free men.'

Herbert Hoover, February 1937.

After the struggle

Because of fears like these Congress turned down the President's plan. Frightened by the threat of reform, however, the Supreme Court began to take a more sympathetic attitude to the laws brought before it. One of the first signs of this came in April 1937, when it upheld the Wagner Act. Shortly afterwards one of the Justices most opposed to the New Deal resigned from the Court and was replaced by a man who favoured reform. From this time onward the Court generally supported the President's policies and so it became unnecessary to appoint additional Justices.

In later years Roosevelt claimed that, in the struggle over the Supreme Court, although he had lost the battle he had won the war. By this he meant that, although he had failed to reform the Court, his actions had forced it to abandon its policy of standing in the way of social reform.

The struggle's effects

In a way this was true, for Roosevelt certainly had little trouble with the Supreme Court from this time onward. In another way, however, he lost a lot by his attempt to 'pack' the Court. Many people who had previously trusted him now began to regard his actions with some suspicion. Perhaps power had gone to his head, they thought.

This new, more watchful attitude caused Roosevelt to be criticised much more widely in the later 1930s than he had been during his first term as President. In the congressional elections which were held in 1938 the Republicans gained many seats. Because of this, and because of growing opposition from conservative Democrats, Roosevelt began to find it more difficult to persuade Congress to pass the laws he wanted. As a result the pace of reform began to slacken.

The New Deal ends

Many people were glad of this. There was a growing feeling that for the time being reform had gone far enough and that it was time to take

A 1937 newspaper cartoon comments on Roosevelt's plans for the Supreme Court. Does the artist approve or disapprove?

a breather. Although few people realised it at the time, the New Deal was practically over by 1938.

The significance of the New Deal

The New Deal's achievements

The New Deal's most obvious achievement was that it had begun to bring the United States out of the Depression. True, there had been a frightening rise in unemployment in the later part of 1937, but this had been checked by another large dose of government spending. Industrial workers, farmers, businessmen – people from almost every section of the community in fact – were better off by the end of 1938 than they had been in the dark days of 1932. Most, though not all, of them gave much of the credit for this improvement to the New Deal.

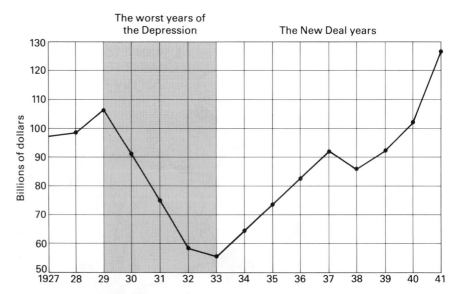

The changes in the gross national product of the USA between 1927 and 1941. This is calculated by adding together the values of all the goods (steel, cars, clothing, etc.) and all the services (catering, transport, etc.) produced in one year. To allow for changes in the value of money all the figures have been calculated in terms of 1929 prices. Note the following points:
1. The steep downward plunge in American income from 1929 to 1933.
2. The rise in income from 1933 onwards.
3. The especially rapid rise in income from 1939 onwards.
Can you give the reasons for these changes?

Government's new role

But the New Deal's achievements went further than this. It altered Americans' ideas about the rightful work of their national government. Before the Depression most had thought of the government as a kind of policeman whose job was simply to keep order. Roosevelt, however, taught Americans to look to the governments they had elected to see that everyone had a fair chance to obtain what he called 'the good things of life'. By doing this, by using the power of the Federal government to ensure fairer treatment for the ordinary citizen, he gave the American people renewed faith in their country's way of life.

Costs

The cost of this achievement was that by the end of the 1930s the Federal government had much more control over the nation's life than it had ever had before. As we have seen already, some people felt that this development threatened the rights of both the individual citizen and the individual state. Others, however, believed that Roosevelt's policies had done more to protect the freedom of the individual than to harm it. They agreed with a claim that Roosevelt himself made a few years later:

'True individual freedom cannot exist without economic security and independence. Necessitous men are not free men. People who are hungry and out of a job are the stuff of which dictatorships are made.'

President Franklin D. Roosevelt, January 1944.

Freedom and dictatorship

The truth of this claim could be judged from events in other lands in the 1930s. In Germany, the Soviet Union and Italy, for example, the problems of the time caused individual rights such as freedom of opinion and of speech to be trampled underfoot by all-powerful dictators whose will became law.

This collapse of democratic freedoms in other countries made the New Deal important beyond the United States. Roosevelt had shown that it was possible to overcome great problems and make beneficial changes in a nation's life without depriving its people of their individual rights. He had shown what 'democracy at work' could do.

PART THREE

THE SECOND WORLD WAR

13

The Gathering Storm: 1931–41

The Good Neighbor and the totalitarian states

When he first became President of the United States, Franklin Roosevelt promised that the United States would follow a policy of friendship towards other countries, a policy which he described as that of 'the good neighbor'.

Latin America

Roosevelt kept this promise, especially towards the USA's neighbours in Central and South America and the Caribbean. He gave up American claims to have the right to interfere in their affairs and withdrew the American troops that for years had been occupying Nicaragua and Haiti. He then organised conferences to improve co-operation between the United States and other American nations. At these conferences arrangements were made about how to encourage trade between them and how to settle disagreements without war.

At first Roosevelt was too busy dealing with the United States' own internal problems to give much attention to events in more distant lands. Soon, however, the aggressive behaviour of certain nations began to force his attention outwards.

Aggression in Asia

First there was Japan, the most industrially and militarily powerful Asian nation. Japan was ruled by an Emperor, Hirohito, but much of the real power there was in the hands of the army. Its generals were eager to bring other lands in Asia under Japanese rule. They believed that this would provide Japan with raw materials and so help to solve the economic problems that it was facing because of the now worldwide depression.

In 1931 the generals had sent Japanese armies marching into Manchuria, an outlying part of Japan's huge but feeble neighbour China. In 1937 Japanese troops attacked the rest of China and by the later part of the year much of the country was under their control.

The United States and Japan

Americans watched the growing power of Japan with anxiety. Many feared that the ambitions of the Japanese stretched beyond China towards the Philippines and the other island territories of the United States in the Pacific – even perhaps beyond the Pacific towards the mainland of America itself.

Mussolini and Abyssinia

Another threat to international peace in the 1930s came from Italy. Its ruler, the dictator Benito Mussolini, wanted to divert the attention of the Italian people from the poverty and unemployment that the depression was causing at home. So in 1935 he sent Italian forces to attack the undeveloped African state of Ethiopia, or Abyssinia. It was a war of tanks and aeroplanes against ancient muzzle-loading guns and the next year the Italians rode in triumph into the Abyssinian capital, Addis Ababa.

Hitler and Germany

But the most serious threat to peace in the 1930s came from Germany. There the hardships of the depression had helped Adolf Hitler, the leader of the Nazi party, to gain power. By 1934 Hitler had destroyed democratic government in Germany and made himself the country's dictator.

For years many Germans had felt that their country had been unjustly treated at the end of the First World War. Hitler now told them that only a strong, ruthless Germany could regain the position in the world which was its right. He built up powerful armed forces and in 1936 ordered German troops to occupy the Rhineland, a German territory along the border with France that the Versailles Treaty had said should remain free of troops. Britain and France took no action to stop him. Encouraged by this, in 1938 Hitler seized Germany's neighbour, Austria. In the following year, despite solemn promises, he swallowed up Czechoslovakia, another of Germany's neighbours.

Totalitarianism

The leaders of Japan, Italy and Germany had certain things in common. They all glorified war as a means of taking people's minds off internal problems. They all taught their peoples to see themselves as members of super races whose right it was to conquer and to rule other nations. And they all believed in totalitarian government, which stamped out rival views by force and regarded individual human beings as of no importance except as servants of the state.

The Axis agreements

In the later 1930s the totalitarian nations drew closer together. In 1936 Hitler and Mussolini signed an agreement setting up what was known as the Rome-Berlin Axis, in which they promised to support one another in quarrels with other nations. In 1937 this Axis agreement was extended to include Japan.

Roosevelt and the dictators

Roosevelt watched the darkening international scene of the 1930s with dismay. He was opposed to everything the totalitarian states stood for – their preaching of racial hatred, suppression of freedom of opinion and of speech, and glorification of war. If he could, he was determined to keep the United States at peace. But he knew that if war came his country might be drawn in whether it wanted to be or not.

A 1938 cartoon shows attacks on world peace. Which countries is the artist accusing?

Roosevelt tried to awaken the American people to this danger. In a speech in 1937 he referred to fighting taking place in China and Europe, and said:

'Without a declaration of war and without warning or justification of any kind, civilians, including vast numbers of women and children, are being ruthlessly murdered by bombs from the air ... innocent peoples, innocent nations are being cruelly sacrificed to a greed for power and supremacy ... If these things come to pass in other parts of the world, let no one imagine that America will escape, that America may expect mercy, that this Western Hemisphere will not be attacked ...'

President Franklin D. Roosevelt, Chicago, October 1937.

Roosevelt ended by hinting that the United States ought to join with other peace-loving nations to stop the spread of violence and aggression in the world.

Opposition to Roosevelt

Roosevelt was deeply disappointed by his countrymen's reaction to his speech. He was accused of being an alarmist, a warmonger and of foolishly trying to involve the United States once more in the troubles in Europe. Even some of the chief supporters of the New Deal were against him, fearing that if the United States became mixed up in overseas problems their plans for more reforms might be pushed aside.

Roosevelt and the isolationists

Why Roosevelt waited

The uproar over his Chicago speech made Roosevelt decide that for the moment it was not practical to try to involve the United States in action against the dictators. Given time, he was convinced that the American people would realise the folly of thinking that they could find safety simply by refusing to join in any such action. But until that moment came he would have to wait. 'It's a terrible thing,' he said later to a friend, 'to look over your shoulder when you're trying to lead – and to find no one there.'

Some people have said since that Roosevelt waited too quietly and too long. They argue that he ought to have made it clear to Hitler and the other dictators that the United States would give support to other democratic nations if they were attacked. Such a stand by the United States in the middle 1930s, they claim, might have made the totalitarian states adopt more peaceful policies.

But Franklin Roosevelt could only act effectively when Congress and the American people were ready to back his actions. He knew that no President could carry out policies which the people were unwilling to support – and in the 1930s most Americans were strongly against their country becoming involved in the troubles of other countries.

Isolationism in the 1930s

The main reason for this was their determination not to get mixed up in any more fighting. The First World War, the 'war to end wars', as Wilson had called it, had been a great disappointment to them. It had cost the United States many lives and a great deal of money. Yet what had been gained? Here the European nations were, it seemed, twenty years later, itching to start fighting all over again. Particularly in the middle and western parts of the United States, most people believed that the best thing for the United States to do this time was to let the Europeans sort out their problems amongst themselves.

Neutrality Acts

As you have read already, people holding this view were known as Isolationists (see page 23). Isolationist influence was very strong in Congress, which from 1935 onwards passed a series of laws called Neutrality Acts. These forbade American citizens to sell military equipment, or to lend money, to nations at war. Even non-military supplies such as foodstuffs could only be sold to such countries if they paid for

The Second World War began in 1939. The cartoonist, like many Americans, wanted the United States to avoid becoming involved.

them on the spot and collected them in their own ships. Congress hoped that this last rule would prevent the United States from being drawn into war as it had been in 1917, by the sinking of its merchant ships while they were carrying goods to warring countries.

Roosevelt was unhappy about the Neutrality Acts. He pointed out that if war came they would make it more difficult for the democratic nations to arm themselves and that this would give a great advantage to the totalitarian states, which already had large stocks of weapons. Congress was determined, however, and the President had to accept the laws.

Preparing for war   But Roosevelt could at least begin to build up the United States' own military strength. The PWA was set to work building aircraft carriers and other ships for the navy. Congress was persuaded to increase the size of the army. As the international situation worsened in the later 1930s, Roosevelt persuaded it to vote still more money for defence.

War comes to Europe

Hitler attacks Poland

On 1 September 1939, the German army attacked Germany's neighbour, Poland. Roosevelt knew that this meant a general war in Europe, for both Britain and France had promised to help Poland if Hitler attacked. On 3 September both countries declared war on Germany. The Second World War had begun.

Cash and Carry

Almost immediately, Roosevelt asked Congress to alter the Neutrality Acts so that Britain and France could be supplied with American arms. Isolationists opposed the change, claiming that such a move would be the first step towards involving the United States in the war. But as the German army and air force smashed Poland into defeat, opinion began to move against them. Eventually Congress approved a new scheme called the Cash and Carry Plan. This allowed Britain and France to buy American war materials so long as they paid for them in cash and carried them away in their own ships.

Hitler attacks again

After Hitler's conquest of Poland an uneasy quiet settled over Europe. Then, in April 1940, Hitler attacked again and occupied neutral Denmark and Norway. In May, German mechanised forces roared into Holland and Belgium and within a week were thrusting deep into northern France. They trapped the main part of the British army and part of the French at the port of Dunkirk. Most of the trapped troops were eventually ferried to safety across the English Channel. But the boats that carried them could only save the men; most of their equipment had to be left behind.

The fall of France

In the first weeks of June Hitler's tanks crushed the remaining French armies and occupied Paris. Sure now that Hitler was going to win, Mussolini decided to join in at the kill. Italian forces invaded France from the south. 'The hand that held the dagger,' commented Roosevelt with contempt, 'has struck it into the back of its neighbor.'

By the end of June 1940 it was all over. France had surrendered and the continent of Europe lay at the feet of the German dictator. Against a military might greater than any in the world, Britain – exhausted and desperately short of weapons – now stood alone.

The United States gets involved

Americans were stunned by Hitler's success. They were alarmed, too. With Hitler the master of Europe and with his ally Japan becoming ever more powerful in Asia, they began to see at last the increasingly dangerous position of their own country, sandwiched between the two.

The 'arsenal of democracy'

Roosevelt drove the lesson home. In the same speech in which he denounced Mussolini's attack on France he painted a frightening picture of a world dominated by force and fear. He stated his determination to 'extend to the opponents of force the material resources of this nation'. There would be no more pretence that the war against Hilter was none of the United States' business:

'The people of Europe who are defending themselves do not ask us to do their fighting. They ask us for the . . . planes, the tanks, the guns, which will enable them to fight for their liberty and for our security. We must get these weapons to them in sufficient [amounts] and quickly enough, so that we and our children will be saved the agony and suffering of war which others have had to endure.

We must be the great arsenal of democracy.'

President Franklin D. Roosevelt, 10 June 1940.

Aid for Britain

Roosevelt began by asking Congress for millions of dollars to strengthen the defences of the United States. But his most urgent task was to get aid to Britain. Even before Dunkirk, the British Prime Minister, Churchill, had sent Roosevelt a long list of things Britain needed. Now the need was desperate.

Roosevelt decided to turn over to the British every scrap of military equipment that the United States could spare, anything that would help them to continue the fight. He 'scraped the bottom of the barrel' so thoroughly that some American troops were soon training with pieces of telephone pole in place of their heavy guns, which had been shipped to England.

Destroyers for bases

To make sure that this equipment reached Britain, Roosevelt gave the British fifty First World War destroyers to help to defend their vital Atlantic supply routes against the attacks of Hitler's U-boats. In return for the destroyers Britain gave the United States the right to set up naval bases on British-owned islands in the Caribbean, guarding the way to the American coast.

Roosevelt's motives

It was not merely sympathy for Britain which made Roosevelt do these things. He was convinced that helping Britain was the best way for the United States to defend itself. Despite fierce criticism of his actions by leading Isolationists, Roosevelt was sure that a majority of the American people now agreed with him. That autumn he was able to test the truth of this belief, for 1940 was Presidential election year.

The 1940 Presidential election

Roosevelt had not at first intended to run for President again. There was a long tradition that no man ought to serve as President for more than two terms.

But if he retired what would happen? On the Democratic side there was no other candidate with his own vote-getting power. What if some isolationist Republican were elected as President? That would mean the end of aid to Britain, the triumph of Hitler and the eventual destruction of the United States. Roosevelt decided that he could not risk this. Tradition or no tradition, he would run again for President.

The voting was closer than in the 1932 and the 1936 elections, but the final outcome was the same. In a moment of crisis even greater than that which they had faced in 1932, the American people again chose Franklin Roosevelt as their President.

The Lend-Lease scheme

How to help Britain

Shortly after his re-election Roosevelt received a message from Churchill. So far most of the equipment that Britain had received from the United States had been obtained under the Cash and Carry Plan worked out a year earlier. But Britain was running out of cash. Churchill warned Roosevelt that his government would soon be unable to pay for any more American supplies.

Roosevelt thought about this problem. Despite the growing sympathy for Britain in the United States, he did not think that Congress would allow him to make the British an outright gift of the things they needed. Nor did he like the idea of lending money. That had been done in the First World War, and afterwards a great deal of ill-feeling had been caused by the inability of the Allied nations to repay the loans.

The answer – Lend-Lease

Then he found the answer. Instead of lending money, why not 'lend' the British the goods themselves? Any left at the war's end could be returned, while any that were destroyed could be regarded as having been used up for the United States' own benefit.

Despite angry attacks by Isolationists, the President's Lend-Lease proposals, as they called, were approved by Congress. Under the Lend-Lease Act of March, 1941, Roosevelt was able to supply military equipment and goods of other kinds to any country whose defence he considered necessary to the safety of the United States.

Lend-Lease for the Russians

The Lend-Lease law was passed to help Britain. But before long another country was in need of American aid. In June 1941, Hitler invaded the Soviet Union. The Russians were driven back everywhere and most American military experts predicted that within a few months their resistance to Hitler would collapse.

Roosevelt was not so sure. He sent Harry Hopkins to see the Soviet leader, Stalin, and weigh up the Russians' chances. When Hopkins returned with an optimistic report Roosevelt decided to give Lend-Lease aid to the Soviet Union, too.

The Atlantic: the Charter and the Battle

Meeting at sea

Early in August 1941, Roosevelt and Churchill met for the first time. Their meeting took place at sea, on board warships anchored off the coast of Newfoundland.

'The Lend-Lease law was mainly intended to help Britain.' Liberator bombers lined up outside the American factory where they have been built, ready to be flown to Britain under the Lend-Lease scheme, August 1941.

The talks between the two leaders covered a wide range of subjects. They discussed ways to make Lend-Lease more effective. They considered how to keep Japan out of the war for as long as possible. They also heard about recent scientific discoveries in the field of nuclear fission and agreed to share information on this important new subject. Already it showed signs of making possible the production of a terrible new weapon – the atomic bomb.

The Atlantic Charter

Before separating, Roosevelt and Churchill drew up a statement which became known as the Atlantic Charter. Its purpose was to make clear the aims which lay behind their countries' resistance to Hitler and to outline their hopes for the future. These were some of the main points of the Charter:

1. Both the United States and Britain promised not to try to increase their own power in the years ahead, either by seizing land belonging to other countries or in any other way.
2. Both agreed that peoples all over the world should be given the right to choose the kind of government under which they wished to live.
3. Both agreed that after 'the final destruction of the Nazi tyranny' the nations of the world should join together to try to ensure peace and greater prosperity for all.

Churchill's opinion of Roosevelt

As the two men parted the British leader thought how fortunate it was for his country that at such a critical time in its history the President of the United States was Franklin Roosevelt. A few years later he summed up his feelings about Roosevelt's actions at this time in these words:

> 'Had he not acted when he did, in the way he did, . . . a hideous fate might well have overwhelmed mankind and made its whole future for centuries sink into shame and ruin. It may well be that he not only anticipated history but altered its course, and altered it in a manner which has saved freedom and earned the gratitude of the human race for generations to come.'
> Winston Churchill, *The Second World War*, 1949.

More aid for Britain

Churchill had good reason for feeling grateful to Roosevelt. By the summer of 1941 American aid to Britain was going much further than providing equipment and supplies. British airmen were being trained in the United States to fight against the might of Hitler's Luftwaffe. British warships were being secretly repaired in American shipyards. Most important of all, the United States' navy had begun to take part in the Battle of the Atlantic.

The Battle of the Atlantic

In the spring of 1941 the Germans were sinking merchant ships bound for Britain twice as fast as new ones could be built. To help to stop this Roosevelt ordered the American navy into action. By July 1941, American destroyers were escorting convoys of merchant ships across the Atlantic as far as Iceland, so that the British only had to guard them for the last part of their dangerous journey. Not surprisingly, the Germans regarded this as being practically the same as the United States joining in the war against them. They struck back with their submarines.

Early in September a U-boat fired on an American destroyer for the first time. Roosevelt replied by ordering American warships to attack first in future.

The Germans accepted the challenge. In October they sank the American destroyer *Reuben James* with the loss of many lives. By the autumn of 1941, although the United States and Germany were officially still at peace, amid the grey waters of the Atlantic war had begun.

14
The United States at War: 1941–44

Pearl Harbor and other defeats

Pearl Harbor, in the Hawaiian Islands, is the American navy's main base in the Pacific Ocean. On the quiet Sunday morning of 7 December 1941, the main part of the United States' Pacific fleet lay at anchor there – battleships, cruisers, destroyers. Only the aircraft carriers were missing, away on a cruise.

Cutting Japan's supplies

Ever since the Japanese army's 1937 attack on China the United States had been reducing exports to Japan of goods that were useful in war – aircraft and chemicals, for example. In July 1941, when Japanese soldiers occupied the French colony of Indochina, it stopped all shipments of oil.

Japan faced disaster. It imported 80 per cent of its oil from the United States. Without this American oil its industries would be paralysed. 'Japan is like a fish in a pond from which the water is being drained away,' a senior naval officer told the Emperor Hirohito.

General Tojo

In October, General Hideki Tojo became Japan's Prime Minister. Tojo knew that there was plenty of oil in the Dutch East Indies (Indonesia). He decided that Japan must seize it. To make it impossible for the American Pacific fleet to interfere with his plans, he ordered a surprise attack on Pearl Harbor.

Pearl Harbor, December 1941

Shortly before 8.00 a.m. on the morning of 7 December, waves of carrier-based Japanese warplanes roared in from the sea and carried out a devastating attack on Pearl Harbor and the neighbouring airfields. The attack took the Americans completely by surprise. Eight of their battleships and a number of other vessels were sunk or seriously damaged, more than two thousand men were killed and hundreds of warplanes were destroyed before they could leave the ground. It was the worst disaster in American naval history.

At the time of the Pearl Harbor attack the United States and Japan were still at peace. They were, in fact, in the middle of negotiations to

'It was the worst disaster in American naval history.' The American battleships West Virginia *and (behind)* Tennessee *on fire and sinking after the Japanese attack on Pearl Harbor, December 1941.*

try to settle their differences. This made the attack particularly shocking to the American people.

The United States declares war

The next day President Roosevelt drove through the rain to ask Congress to declare war on Japan. In a short speech, delivered in a tone of cold, contemptuous anger, he described 7 December as 'a date that will live in infamy'. With only one opposing vote Congress granted his request, and declared war on Japan.

Two days later Roosevelt spoke again, this time over the radio to the American people. Here is part of what he said:

'In the past few years – and most violently in the past few days – we have learned a terrible lesson . . . We must begin the great task that is before us by abandoning once for all the illusion that we can ever again isolate ourselves from the rest of humanity . . . there is no such thing as security for any nation – or any individual – in a world ruled by the principles of gangsterism. There is no such thing as impregnable defence against powerful aggressors who sneak up in the dark and strike without warning. We have learned that . . . we cannot measure our safety in terms of miles on any map . . .'

President Franklin D. Roosevelt, radio broadcast,
10 December, 1941.

Planning for Allied victory

On 22 December 1941, Winston Churchill flew to meet Roosevelt in Washington. By now the United States was at war with Germany and Italy too, for they had declared war on the Americans in support of their ally Japan on 11 December.

Roosevelt and Churchill made two especially important decisions at their Washington meeting. The first was to set up a special group of American and British military and naval experts called the Combined Chiefs of Staff to work out joint plans for defeating their enemies. The second decision was even more important.

Despite the fact that Americans understandably felt more anger towards Japan than towards Germany, Roosevelt and Churchill agreed that the United States and Britain must concentrate upon defeating Hitler first. Germany was the most powerful Axis nation and might still be strong enough to win the war even if Japan were defeated. If Germany were defeated, however, the two leaders were confident that Japan could soon be dealt with.

War in the Pacific

The months which followed the Washington meeting were gloomy ones for the Allies. In the early part of 1942 the forces of Japan swept over south-east Asia and the islands of the western Pacific. Within a few months they had conquered over 2.5 million square kilometres of land and brought more than 100 million people under their rule. The newly-conquered lands were rich in raw materials such as tin and oil, which added greatly to the military strength of Japan. By the summer Japanese armies were threatening India and Australia. The extent of the Japanese conquests is shown on the map on page 108.

War in the Soviet Union

The war against the Germans was going badly for the Allies, too. In a new offensive in the spring of 1942 Hitler's armies smashed deeper into the vast territories of the Soviet Union. Many experts began to fear that Russian resistance to Hitler might collapse unless more were done to help them.

War in North Africa

The Germans were on the attack in North Africa, too. The armoured columns of a brilliant general named Rommel were threatening Egypt, the main centre of British power in the oil-rich Middle East. The British eventually halted Rommel, but no one knew how long they would be able to hold him. They were in great need of equipment, especially tanks and heavy guns.

War in the Atlantic

Finally there was bad news from the Atlantic, where German submarines seemed to be winning control of the seaways. The Germans had moved all the U-boats they could into the Atlantic, in order to choke off the flow of American supplies to Britain and the Middle East. Some were prowling along the American coast, torpedoing merchant ships silhouetted against the lights of coastal cities. Others formed 'wolf packs', groups of submarines which hunted down their prey together. In the first six months of 1942 these wolf packs sank 506 Allied merchant ships for the loss of only 28 of their own number.

Producing for war

Conscription

Over a year before the entry of the United States into the war Roosevelt had persuaded Congress to pass a law authorising the conscription of young men for military service. This had made it possible to start increasing the number of men in the American armed forces. After Pearl Harbor this recruitment of fighting men was speeded up.

But all the nations involved in the Second World War knew that it would eventually be won by the side which produced the most tanks, the most aircraft and the most other weapons. The war was as much a contest between the factories of the warring nations as between their fighting forces.

American war reserves

On the Allied side the United States had a particularly important part to play. By 1942 many of the Soviet Union's industrial areas were occupied by the Germans, while those of Britain were under frequent air attacks. United States' factories were beyond the range of enemy attacks and so were able to work unhindered. Not only this, but it had more factories suitable for producing war supplies, and more of the necessary raw materials, than any other country in the world. In 1942 both Britain and the Soviet Union were looking to these American factories to provide them with vitally needed equipment.

Organising the economy

The United States did not let its allies down. The government organised the country's whole economy towards winning the war. It placed controls on wages and prices, and introduced high income taxes. It rationed gasoline and some foods. It also spent a vast amount – two thousand million dollars – on a top-secret research scheme. The scheme was code-named the Manhattan Project. By 1945 scientists working on the scheme had produced and tested the world's first atomic bomb.

Producing for war

Even before the attack on Pearl Harbor the production of war supplies by American factories had risen considerably. During 1941 the output of munitions had more than doubled, and by the time Pearl Harbor was attacked aircraft were being produced at a rate equal to 25,000 a year. Yet even this was not enough to meet the needs of a worldwide war. Roosevelt laid down massive new production targets for 1942. These included 60,000 aircraft and 45,000 tanks.

The War Production Board

At first there was some confusion, especially over the allocation of supplies of raw materials. But guided by a new government agency called the War Production Board (WPB), American industry quickly settled down to its task. New factories were built, often with amazing speed. Unemployment practically disappeared as both men and women flocked to work in them. Existing factories abandoned the production of peacetime goods such as refrigerators and washing machines, and turned instead to making tanks, aeroplanes and other war supplies. In the huge plants of manufacturers like the Ford Company, bombers instead of cars now rolled off the production lines.

Solving shortages

Occasionally shortages of vital parts or of raw materials held back production. When this happened the WPB organised immediate attempts to find ways round the difficulty. When a shortage of certain kinds of electrical equipment held up the building of merchant ships, for instance, a completely new ship was designed which did not need the scarce components. This was named the 'Liberty' ship. Hundreds of these ugly little vessels were built to keep supplies flowing across the oceans to the United States' allies. A little later a shortage of rubber was met by the setting up of enormous new factories to produce synthetic rubber.

The 'arsenal of democracy'

The total amounts of war materials produced by American factories were enormous. As early as 1942 they were producing more than all the factories of the Axis powers combined. By the end of the war in 1945 they had produced 86,330 tanks, 296,400 aeroplanes, 64,500 landing craft, 6,500 naval vessels and 5,400 cargo ships and transports.

American-built fighter aircraft appeared in the skies of Britain, helping to drive back German bombers; American-built tanks were sent to the Soviet Union and Egypt to halt the advance of Hitler's armies. The United States had become what Roosevelt had earlier promised it would become – 'the arsenal of democracy'.

Turning the tide against Germany

By the summer of 1942 the Allies were ready to hit back at Hitler. The German dictator's empire now covered most of Europe and part of North Africa. The problem facing the Allies was where to attack it.

Europe or Africa?

The Americans favoured an early attack on western Europe. Roosevelt was anxious about the possible collapse of the Soviet Union, and his generals believed that the quickest way to defeat Hitler would be to strike hard through France, right at the heart of Germany. The British disagreed. Churchill believed that the Allies needed to be stronger in both men and equipment before they could hope to make such an attack successfully.

Churchill suggested that an invasion force should be sent instead to North Africa. This, he claimed, would force Hitler to send reinforcements there and so reduce German pressure on the Soviet armies. In addition such an attack would give valuable battle experience to the so far inexperienced American troops.

Operation Torch, 1942

Roosevelt had doubts about Churchill's suggestion. His advisers thought that it was motivated more by Churchill's desire to protect Britain's interests in Egypt and the Middle East than by the other reasons he had given. Nevertheless, Roosevelt accepted the plan. It was given the code name of Operation Torch. Since the United States would be providing many of the men and most of the equipment for it, an American general named Eisenhower was appointed to take command.

Victory in North Africa

Early in November American and British troops landed in Morocco and Algeria in North Africa. They met only scattered resistance and were soon moving rapidly eastwards. At the other end of North Africa Rommel was already in full retreat across the Libyan Desert after a heavy defeat by the British Eighth Army under General Montgomery at the Battle of El Alamein.

A few months later Eisenhower's forces from Morocco and Montgomery's from Egypt met in Tunisia. In the middle of May 1943, the German forces in North Africa surrendered.

The Casablanca Conference, 1943

The previous January President Roosevelt had flown secretly to North Africa to meet Churchill. After discussions in the recently-occupied city of Casablanca, the two leaders announced their determination to fight on until the Axis governments surrendered without conditions.

This demand for what was called 'unconditional surrender' was mainly Roosevelt's idea, and was intended to reassure Stalin. The Soviet leader had been angered by the decision to invade North Africa instead of Europe, suspecting that Roosevelt and Churchill wanted the Soviet armies to shoulder the chief burden of fighting the Germans. The unconditional surrender demand was intended to convince him that his American and British allies would not make a separate peace with Hitler, but would see the war through to the end.

Italy surrenders

In July 1943, American and British troops from North Africa crossed the Mediterranean Sea and landed in Sicily, the large island at the toe of Italy.

As the Allied armies swept through Sicily, Mussolini was overthrown and a new government took power. Early in September, as Allied troops moved across the narrow straits which separate Sicily from the Italian mainland, this new government surrendered unconditionally.

This did not mean the end of fighting in Italy, for large German armies still occupied most of the country. Long months of fierce and bloody warfare lay ahead as the Americans and British fought their way northwards up the Italian peninsula.

The Quebec Conference, 1943

Meanwhile, in August, Churchill and Roosevelt had met again. In the Canadian city of Quebec they had agreed upon a plan for the attack which they hoped would finally finish Hitler – the invasion of western Europe. The plan was given the code name of Operation Overlord. General Eisenhower was chosen later as its Supreme Commander.

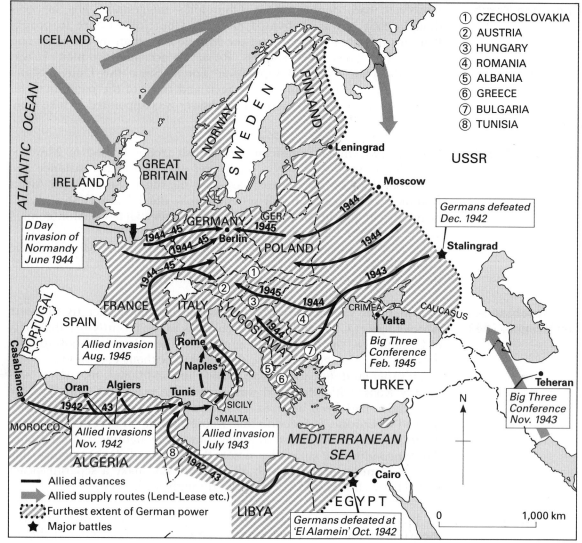

The Second World War in Europe and North Africa (1942–45).

Map labels:
- ① CZECHOSLOVAKIA
- ② AUSTRIA
- ③ HUNGARY
- ④ ROMANIA
- ⑤ ALBANIA
- ⑥ GREECE
- ⑦ BULGARIA
- ⑧ TUNISIA

ICELAND · ATLANTIC OCEAN · IRELAND · GREAT BRITAIN · NORWAY · SWEDEN · FINLAND · USSR · Leningrad · Moscow · GERMANY · GER. · Berlin · POLAND · Stalingrad · Germans defeated Dec. 1942 · D Day invasion of Normandy June 1944 · FRANCE · ITALY · YUGOSLAVIA · CRIMEA · Yalta · CAUCASUS · PORTUGAL · SPAIN · Allied invasion Aug. 1945 · Rome · Naples · Big Three Conference Feb. 1945 · TURKEY · Teheran · Big Three Conference Nov. 1943 · Casablanca · Oran · Algiers · Tunis · SICILY · MALTA · MOROCCO · Allied invasions Nov. 1942 · Allied invasion July 1943 · MEDITERRANEAN SEA · Cairo · ALGERIA · LIBYA · EGYPT · Germans defeated at 'El Alamein' Oct. 1942

Legend:
- Allied advances
- Allied supply routes (Lend-Lease etc.)
- Furthest extent of German power
- ★ Major battles

N · 0 · 1,000 km

The tide turns

By the autumn of 1943 the news from the war fronts was good. In Italy the Allied armies captured the city of Naples. In the Soviet Union the Germans were being pushed back by a series of massive Russian attacks. In east Asia and the Pacific the Japanese advances had been halted and they were now being forced on to the defensive. The Battle of the Atlantic was being won, too. With the development of radar and other new weapons many more U-boats were being destroyed, while the losses of Allied shipping were only a fraction of what they had been in the previous year.

Preparations for Overlord

In this same autumn of 1943 the British and American air forces were mounting massive round-the-clock bombing attacks on Germany's cities and industries. One of the main aims of the raids was to weaken the Germans in preparation for the invasion of France the following summer.

All through the winter and the following spring there was a massive build-up of men and equipment in Britain. By the beginning of June 1944, all was ready. Early in the morning of 6 June – D-Day – the long awaited Overlord Invasion began.

D-Day, June 1944 The first landings took place on the coast of Normandy in northern France. While Allied aircraft and battleships kept up a heavy bombardment of the German defences, men and equipment poured ashore from an invasion fleet which stretched as far as the eye could see.

The battle for Normandy Within two weeks of the first landings the Allies put a million men and their equipment on to the Normandy beaches. When they recovered from their surprise, the Germans fought fiercely to pen in the Allied forces along the coast. For some weeks they succeeded. Then, in the last week of July, Allied soldiers smashed through the German defences and raced deep inland.

The German retreat To avoid being trapped the German armies fell back to the frontiers of their own country, where a last line of defence had been prepared. By the middle of September they had been driven from almost all of France and Belgium, and the first Allied troops were standing on the soil of Germany itself.

The Russians, too, were now pressing the Germans hard. By the autumn they had driven them out of the Soviet Union and were pushing onwards through central Europe to Germany's eastern borders. By the end of the year an iron ring was tightening round Hitler. Although his armies were still fighting back desperately, the end of the war in Europe was in sight.

Turning the tide against Japan

Japanese advances, 1942 In the first half of 1942, the victorious Japanese built up a big empire in South-East Asia and amongst the islands of the Pacific Ocean. By the summer of 1942 their armies were pushing through the jungles of Burma towards India, the main Asian territory of the British Empire. To the south they were moving along the northern coasts of New Guinea to threaten Australia. To the east and north they were planning sea-borne attacks in the direction of the Hawaiian and Aleutian Islands. The full extent of the Japanese advances can be seen on the map on page 108.

Coral Sea and Midway, 1942 In May 1942, Allied leaders received the first encouraging news from the Pacific. In the Battle of the Coral Sea warplanes from American aircraft carriers heavily damaged a Japanese invasion force heading for the Allied base of Port Moresby in New Guinea. A month later came

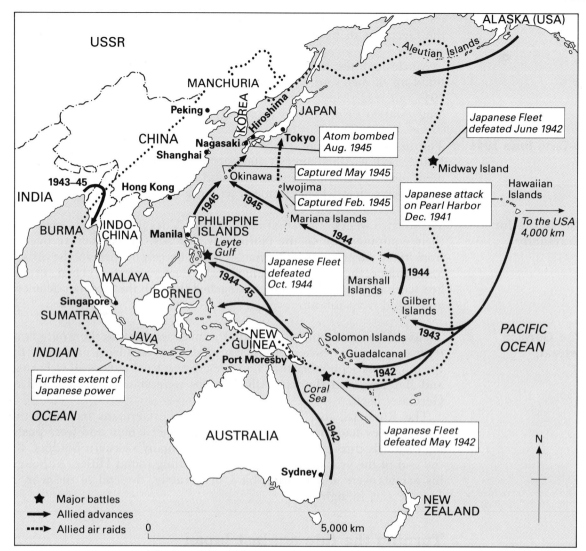

The Second World War in the Pacific (1941–45).

more cheering news. The greater part of the Japanese navy headed for the important American base of Midway Island, which guarded the approach to the Hawaiian Islands. Again the Japanese were intercepted by American aircraft and turned back with heavy losses.

New Guinea and Guadalcanal

In the months which followed the Coral Sea and Midway battles, American and Australian land forces under the American General Douglas MacArthur began pushing back the Japanese armies. The first objective was to drive them out of New Guinea and the other advanced bases from which they were threatening Australia. One of the most important of these was Guadalcanal in the Solomon Islands. After six months of bloody fighting, the Japanese were eventually forced to abandon both New Guinea and Guadalcanal at the beginning of 1943.

Allied plans

By now the Americans and their Australian and British allies had agreed upon their long-term plan for the defeat of the Japanese. They decided upon a three-pronged attack.

From the base in Australia one prong was to push northwards towards Japan through the Philippine Islands. From the base in Hawaii another prong was to strike westwards towards Japan through the islands of the central Pacific. Finally, the Pacific offensives would be backed up by a drive through Burma into Malaya and the other lands which the Japanese had conquered in South-East Asia.

By June 1943, the Pacific offensives were under way. American forces advanced towards Japan by 'island hopping' – that is, by capturing Japanese-held islands that made good bases from which to advance still further, while by-passing others.

Allied advances, 1943–44

By the end of the year the outermost ring of Japanese defensive bases had been cracked open and throughout 1944 the Allies fought their way nearer and nearer to Japan itself. In June an enormous American task force gained control of the important Mariana Islands. By the autumn the British were driving the Japanese back through Burma. In October American troops returned to the Philippine Islands, and so cut the main supply route between Japan and its conquests in South-East Asia. All these moves can be seen on the map on page 108.

By the end of 1944 Japan itself had come within range of Allied air attacks. From November onward the palm-fringed airstrips of newly-captured islands roared to the sound of American heavy bombers taking off to attack its cities and industries. As the two prongs of the Pacific offensive met and overlapped, the Allies made ready for the final strike at Japan.

15
Preparing a Peace and Ending a War: 1943–45

The Big Three at Teheran, 1943

At the end of their Quebec meeting in August 1943, Churchill and Roosevelt invited the Soviet leader, Stalin, to meet them. They wanted to work out joint plans for the final defeat of the Axis powers. Stalin accepted the invitation, but refused to come any further outside the Soviet Union than Teheran, the capital of the Soviet Union's neighbour Iran.

Planning for war

The three leaders met in November 1943. The main topic of their meetings was how to speed the defeat of Germany. Churchill still believed that an invasion of western Europe was not the best way to achieve this. Roosevelt and Stalin insisted on such an attack, however. An invasion in the west would force Hitler to withdraw men and supplies from the Soviet Union, where the soldiers of the Red Army were suffering heavy losses as they drove the Germans step by step from their land. Churchill had to give way and the United States and Britain promised to launch Operation Overlord by the following June. Stalin then hinted that when the Germans were defeated he would turn the Soviet armies eastwards and help his allies to defeat Japan, with whom the Soviet Union was so far still at peace.

Planning for peace

Problems of the future were also considered by the 'Big Three'. There was the question of what should happen to the countries of Europe once they had been freed from Hitler's domination; of what should happen to Germany itself; most important of all, of how to avoid wars and ensure international co-operation in the years ahead. These were difficult problems, but Roosevelt believed that with trust and goodwill, especially between himself and Stalin, they could be solved.

Communism and capitalism

Stalin was the difficulty. The Soviet leader was a communist, which meant that his ideas about government and the way in which society should be organised were very different from those of Roosevelt and

Churchill. For example, in economic affairs he and other communists believed that a nation's industry and agriculture should be owned and controlled by the state on behalf of the people as a whole. The United States and Britain, on the other hand, were capitalist countries – that is, countries whose economic way of life was based upon industry and agriculture being owned by private individuals. Politically, too, the Soviet Union was very different from Britain and the United States. Its communist rulers refused to allow anyone to share their power or to hold views which were different from their own. In fact, the Soviet Union under Stalin was just as much of a totalitarian state as was Germany under Hitler.

Stalin's suspicions   Stalin's ideas about the future also differed from those of Roosevelt and Churchill. Communists believed that conflict and enmity between capitalist countries and their own were inevitable. Stalin was especially suspicious of the United States and Britain, the two strongest capitalist countries. He believed that only the need to defeat Hitler had made them friendly towards the Soviet Union and that their friendship would not last. Once the war was over, he believed, they might well turn

'Roosevelt believed that some sort of agreement might be reached with the Soviet leader if only he could win his trust and friendship.' Roosevelt and Stalin share a joke, but Churchill looks glum. Teheran Conference, November 1943.

against his country and try to crush its communist way of life, as Britain and other countries had done after the First World War.

Roosevelt and Stalin

Roosevelt knew about Stalin's suspicions, but with his usual optimism thought that he could reach some sort of agreement with the Soviet leader. What was important, he believed, was to reassure Stalin about the future security of the Soviet Union and to win his trust and friendship. So he agreed to the Soviet Union moving its frontier with Poland further west. He made fun of Churchill, deliberately teasing him so that the Soviet leader would not feel that he was an outsider. By the end of the Teheran conference he was sure that he had succeeded in achieving his aims. 'I may say that I got along fine with Marshal Stalin,' he told the American people when he returned, '. . . and I believe that we are going to get along very well with him and the Russian people – very well indeed.'

Time would show that he was mistaken.

Preparations for peace

Towards the end of 1944, with the war almost won, Roosevelt became increasingly concerned with preparing for the coming peace.

The 'Four Freedoms'

Long before this he had described four basic objectives which he hoped to see achieved when the war was over:

> 'In the future days, which we seek to make secure, we look forward to a world founded on (1) freedom of speech and expression, everywhere in the world; (2) freedom of every person to worship God in his own way, everywhere in the world; (3) freedom from want for every nation; (4) freedom from fear for every nation . . .'
>
> President Franklin D. Roosevelt, 6 January, 1941.

But Roosevelt knew that these 'Four Freedoms' and the aims set out later that year in the Atlantic Charter (see page 98) would only be achieved by careful preparation and planning. The first step, he believed, was to set up an effective organisation to bring about co-operation between the nations of the world.

The United Nations Organisation

Long before the United States entered the war, therefore, Roosevelt encouraged his Secretary of State, Cordell Hull, the man most concerned in helping him with foreign affairs, to make enquiries about the possibility of forming such an organisation once the war had been won. Remembering President Wilson's failure to persuade Congress to support United States' membership of the League of Nations after the First World War, he took care to include leading Republicans in this planning for the peace.

In March, 1943, both houses of Congress voted for the United States to take the lead in founding what came to be called, at Roosevelt's suggestion, the United Nations Organisation. In the months which followed, the UNO idea was discussed with Britain and the Soviet Union. Both supported it and agreed that there should be a conference at Dumbarton Oaks, near Washington, to work out the first details.

The Dumbarton Oaks Conference, 1944

In August 1944, delegates from the United States, Britain, the Soviet Union and China worked out an outline plan for the new organisation. It seemed that an important step had been taken towards achieving what Roosevelt wanted – 'a peace that will last, and a peace in which the . . . larger nations will work absolutely in unison in preventing war.'

UNRRA

The following November one of the first of many UNO agencies was set up. This was the United Nations Relief and Rehabilitation Administration. UNRRA's job was to supply food, clothing and other necessities to the people of those parts of the world which had been devastated by the war.

Roosevelt's last election, 1944

In the autumn of 1944 the latest news from the war fronts began to share the headlines of American newspapers with another important topic – the approaching Presidential election.

For the fourth successive time Franklin Roosevelt was chosen as the candidate of the Democratic party. He had mixed feelings about running again. The strain of his twelve hectic years of office was beginning to tell. 'All that is within me cries to go back to my house on the Hudson,' he wrote when he was chosen.

But Roosevelt believed that he could not do this. There was a war to be won and after that a peace to be made secure. He felt that he had no more right to give up now than had the soldiers at the battlefronts.

Roosevelt and Dewey

Roosevelt's Republican opponent was Thomas Dewey, the Governor of New York State. Because of the great prestige that the President had earned by his war leadership, Dewey faced a difficult job in trying to defeat him. Nevertheless, the Republicans were hopeful. In the congressional elections two years earlier they had made large gains. By abandoning their earlier policies of isolationism and opposition to social reform, and by painting Roosevelt as a 'tired old man', the Republicans thought that they could win.

At first it looked as if they might be right. That summer Roosevelt visited the Hawaiian and the Aleutian Islands to see for himself how the war in the Pacific was going and to meet the Commanders there to discuss plans for the final assault on Japan. When he returned to America he stood on the windswept deck of the battle cruiser which had brought him home to give an account of his journey.

The trip had been a strenuous one for the sixty-two-year-old President and he was tired. In addition he was in considerable pain from his leg-braces, which he was wearing for the first time in months to enable him to give his speech from a standing position. He struggled through the speech, but it left many people with an uneasy feeling – was this tired and obviously ageing man really strong enough to stand the strain of being President for another four years?

Winning a fourth term

Roosevelt himself was sure that he was, but he knew that he had to convince the voters of this. By the end of September he had regained some of his old form. The climax to his campaign came when he drove for four hours in an open car through the streets of New York. It rained heavily all the time, an icy downpour which soaked him to the skin, but he refused to give up the drive. 'I was really worried about him that day,' said his wife, 'but instead of being completely exhausted he was exhilarated.' The cheering crowds acted like a tonic on the President. 'I felt the crowd,' he said. 'I felt as though I belonged to them and they belonged to me. It kept me warm and I didn't know I was wet through.'

The drive through New York convinced many doubters that Roosevelt was fit enough to serve for another term. Once this had been achieved, his international reputation and his promise to return to the New Deal after the war proved a winning combination. In the election in November he defeated Dewey comfortably.

The Big Three at Yalta, 1945

By the time Roosevelt took the oath of office as President for the fourth time on 20 January 1945, the Allied armies in Europe were close to victory. Almost everywhere Hitler's armies had been driven back on to German soil. In the Pacific Allied forces were approaching nearer and nearer to the home islands of Japan.

With the war clearly in its last stages, Roosevelt became ever more concerned with the problem of how to achieve a lasting peace. The answer, he still believed, was to ensure that the wartime co-operation between the United States, Britain and the Soviet Union continued when the war was over.

The Yalta Conference, 1945

A few days after his inauguration Roosevelt left Washington on yet another long journey. His destination was the Crimea in the south of the Soviet Union, where another conference had been arranged between himself, Churchill and Stalin.

Roosevelt arrived in Yalta, the seaside town where the conference was to meet, on 3 February 1945. Many who saw him at Yalta, and millions more who saw newsreel films of the conference later, were shocked by the change in his appearance. His face was haggard and he had lost so much weight that his clothes no longer fitted him properly. His hands, which had always had a slight tremor, now shook so badly that he could hardly light the cigarettes that he smoked constantly.

'His face was haggard and he had lost so much weight his clothes no longer fitted him.' Roosevelt with Churchill, Yalta Conference, February, 1945.

Decisions at Yalta
The Big Three made a number of important decisions at Yalta. Here is a list of some of them:

1. Final agreement was reached upon how best to finish off the war against Hitler.
2. Arrangements were made to divide Germany after the end of the fighting into a number of zones, each of which would be occupied by the forces of one of the Allies.
3. Stalin agreed that within two to three months of the defeat of Hitler the Soviet Union would declare war on Japan.
4. The peoples of the countries which were being freed from Hitler's grasp were promised that they would be given the chance to choose for themselves the kind of government they wanted.
5. Agreement was reached on voting rights and other matters relating to the United Nations Organisation, and it was agreed that a conference should be held in San Francisco in April to settle the final details.

Disappointed hopes
Roosevelt returned from Yalta well satisfied with what had been achieved. Both he and Churchill were hopeful that when the war was

over the Soviet Union would continue to work in friendly co-operation with their own countries.

Their hopes were soon dashed. At the time of the Yalta Conference it had seemed that the war against Germany might stretch well into 1945. Within weeks of the end of the Conference, however, it became clear that German resistance was beginning to crumble and that the final collapse was only weeks away. With the war almost over, Stalin's reasons for friendship and co-operation with his allies were fast disappearing.

Stalin's attitude

Despite Roosevelt's attempts to win him over, the Russian dictator still believed that there could be no lasting friendship between his own country and the United States and Britain. The most important thing to Stalin in the years ahead was not the need to continue to co-operate with his wartime allies; it was the need to ensure that the Soviet Union was strong in case they turned hostile.

The President's last days

Disappointment in Eastern Europe

In the early spring of 1945 there were more and more signs that Stalin had no intention of keeping one of the key promises that he had made at Yalta. As the Soviet armies drove the Germans out of Eastern Europe, he made sure that Russian-controlled governments were set up in country after country there.

By the middle of March Churchill was already writing to tell Roosevelt how dismayed he was at the 'great failure and . . . utter breakdown of what was settled at Yalta'. Roosevelt shared Churchill's dismay and cabled that he, too, was 'watching with anxiety and concern the development of the Soviet attitude'. He feared that the increasing hostility of Stalin was endangering the hopes of people everywhere for a better and more peaceful world in the years ahead.

Hopes for the UN

But one great hope remained – the United Nations Organisation. The conference to settle its final shape was due to begin in San Francisco at the end of April and Roosevelt intended to be there to open it in person.

Failing health

But first he had to rest. The draining away of his physical strength which had shown at Yalta was now even more marked. At the end of March Roosevelt left Washington for a few weeks of relaxation at a health resort called Warm Springs in the southern state of Georgia.

Most afternoons the President went for slow, rambling drives through the Georgia countryside and within a few days some of his old vigour returned. By the morning of 12 April he was feeling well enough to pose for a painter who was doing his portrait. Wearing a dark blue suit and a red tie, he sat in the leather armchair by the fireplace of his cottage reading a batch of reports.

Roosevelt dies. Headlines in New York City newspapers, April, 1945.

**Roosevelt's
death: April 1945**

Suddenly he groaned. He pressed his hand to his temple and rubbed
it hard, then fell back unconscious in his chair. He had suffered a
stroke. He was carried to his bedroom, where he lived, breathing
heavily but without regaining consciousness, for another four hours.
Late in the afternoon he died.

The news was sent to Mrs Roosevelt in Washington and she cabled
it to their four sons. Soon the nation and the world knew. When they
saw the newspaper headlines grown men and women wept in the
streets, for they felt that they had lost a close and valued friend. When
Churchill heard he felt as if someone had struck him a heavy blow. 'I
was overpowered by a sense of deep and irreparable loss,' he wrote
later.

But perhaps the most moving tribute came from an unknown soldier.
Frances Perkins described the incident:

'On the night he died a young soldier stood in the silent group which
clustered for comfort around the White House where he had lived.

> The young soldier sighed as I nodded to him and still looking at the
> house, he said: "I felt as if I knew him." [A pause] "I felt as if he
> knew me – and I felt as if he liked me."'
>
> Frances Perkins, *The Roosevelt I Knew*, 1949.

Roosevelt's funeral

The next day the President's body was taken back to Washington and driven through packed but silent streets to the White House. A brief service was held there and on the following day the funeral procession began the last stage of its journey to Hyde Park, where the President had asked to be buried. Here, as a breeze from the Hudson stirred the trees, and to the slow beat of muffled drums, the coffin was lowered into the grave. The President was home.

The last days of war

President Truman

Roosevelt was succeeded as President by Harry S. Truman, the man who five months earlier had been elected to serve with him as Vice-President. Truman said later that he felt as if the heavens had fallen upon him, but he quickly settled in to the task of continuing Roosevelt's work.

Germany surrenders

Within two weeks of the death of President Roosevelt, American and British troops advancing eastwards met Soviet forces moving westwards on the banks of the River Elbe in the centre of Germany. A week later Hitler shot himself in an underground shelter in Berlin and in the days which followed the German armies everywhere laid down their arms. The final German surrender came on 7 May. On the following day bonfires blazed all over Europe and America, and people danced and sang in the streets in celebration of the end of the war in Europe.

Okinawa

There still remained the task of defeating the Japanese. By August American forces had captured the island of Okinawa, only 350 miles from the coast of Japan. The Japanese had defended the island with suicidal courage and its capture cost the Americans 50,000 casualties. The same sort of bitter fighting seemed to await them when they invaded Japan.

Hiroshima: August 1945

But the invasion never came. On 16 July 1945, Allied scientists working on the Manhattan Project (see page 103) successfully exploded an atomic bomb, the most terribly destructive weapon mankind had ever seen. An ultimatum was sent to the Japanese demanding their immediate surrender, but military leaders forced the government to ignore it. To avoid the great loss of lives which an invasion seemed certain to cost, President Truman ordered an atomic bomb to be dropped on Japan.

At fifteen minutes past eight on the morning of 6 August an American bomber flew over the city of Hiroshima and dropped the bomb. Forty-five seconds later it exploded, and a mushroom-shaped cloud climbed high into the sky above the doomed city. The explosion's effect on Hiroshima was described by the head of a Japanese investigating team:

'I arrived about five-thirty in the evening. When the plane flew over Hiroshima there was but one black dead tree, as if a crow was perched on it. There was nothing there but that tree. As we landed at the airport all the grass was red as if it had been toasted. There was no fire any more. Everything had burnt up simultaneously. Some schools with blown-off roofs and broken windows were left standing at some distance from the center of the city. But the city itself was completely wiped out. That must be the word, yes, completely wiped out.'

General Seizo Arisue, quoted in L. Giovanitti and F. Freed, *The Decision to Drop the Bomb, 1967.*

An official American report estimated that seventy to eighty thousand people were killed at Hiroshima and an equal number injured.

The war ends   Three days later a second atomic bomb was dropped on the city of Nagasaki, and on 14 August the Japanese government agreed to surrender. The official documents were signed aboard the American battleship *Missouri* on 2 September. The Second World War was over.

Verdict

In 1960, fifteen years after Franklin Roosevelt's death, the American magazine *Look* printed an article about him. In the weeks following many of the magazine's readers wrote letters to its editor about the article:

'Thanks for the greatest article on the greatest American of my time,' wrote one reader. 'A moving account of this wonderful man's life,' wrote another. 'Superb!' wrote yet another.

The reaction of other readers was different. 'No American individual in the past half century has done this country such incalculable harm,' wrote one. 'He's dead. Why not leave him that way?' wrote another.

Somewhere in between these very different sets of opinions about Roosevelt comes this, written by a journalist on *The New York Times* newspaper in 1979:

'Franklin Delano Roosevelt had no equal among American presidents in the acquisition, use and enjoyment of political power. His basic purposes were always noble, although his means were occasionally less so. By applying his particular skills in a thoroughly pragmatic [practical] approach to the awesome problems of his presidency, he brought capitalism in the United States back from the brink and then led his country into a crusade that saved democracy for another chance in the world.'

Turner Cartledge, *Portraits of Power*, 1979.

That is one person's summing up of the importance of Franklin Roosevelt. What would yours be?

Index

Acknowledgements

We are grateful to Warner Chappell Music Ltd for permission to reproduce the lyrics of 'Brother Can You Spare A Dime' by Gorney & Harburg. © Harms Inc.

We have been unable to trace the copyright holders of 'Working Man Blues' by Sleepy John Estes, 'CIO Union Song' and 'The Mining Town' by Aunt Molly Jackson, and would appreciate any information which would enable us to do so.

We are grateful to the following for permission to reproduce photographs: Associated Press, page 47; The Bettmann Archive, pages 19, 35, 37, 87, 101; Culver Pictures, pages 5, 16, 21, 56; Food Motor Company Ltd, page 29; The Granger Collection, pages 7, 94; Imperial War Museum, page 98; Library of Congress, pages 75, 84; *New York Daily News*, page 62; Popperfoto, pages 45, 76, 111; Franklin D. Roosevelt Library, pages 3, 42 (Wide World Photos), 50 (Detroit News), 60 (Philadelphia Record), 67 (New York World Telegram), 115, 117; Tennessee Valley Authority, page 70.

We are unable to locate the copyright holders of the following and would be grateful for any information that would enable us to do so: pages 24, 30, 38, 72, 92.

Cover: Franklin D. Roosevelt addressing the nation over the radio in one of his 'fireside chats'; photo: The Bettmann Archive.

Longman Group UK Limited
Longman House, Burnt Mill, Harlow,
Essex CM20 2JE, England
and Associated Companies throughout the world.

Published in the United States of America
by Longman Inc., New York

First published 1966
Second edition 1991
Second impression 1992

ISBN 0 582 08008 8

Set in 11/12pt Baskerville Roman (Linotron 202)

Produced by Longman Singapore Publishers (Pte) Ltd
Printed in Singapore

British Library Cataloguing in Publication Data
O'Callaghan, D. B. (Dennis Brynley) *1931–*
    Roosevelt and the United States. – 2nd. ed. – (Modern times)
    1. Politics. United States. Roosevelt, Franklin D.
    (Franklin Delano) 1882–1945
    I. Title II. Series
    973.9179092
    ISBN 0-582-08008-8

Library of Congress Cataloging in Publication Data
O'Callaghan, D. B.
    Roosevelt and the United States/D. B. O'Callaghan. – 2nd. ed.
    p.   cm. – (Modern times)
    Includes index.
    Summary: Describes political events in this country during
Franklin D. Roosevelt's life and administration..
    ISBN 0-582-08008-8
    1. United States – Politics and government – 1933-1945
2. Roosevelt, Franklin D. (Franklin Delano), 1882-1945.   3. United
States – Hisroty – 20th century.   [1. United States – Politics and
government – 1933-1945   2. Roosevelt, Franklin D. (Franklin Delano),
1882 – 1945.   3. United States – Hisroty – 20th century.]   I. Title
II. Series: Modern times (Harlow, England)
    E806.042   1991
    973.917 – dc20

The publisher's policy to use paper manufactured from
sustainable forests.